Patrolling the Heart of the Silver State

More True Tales from a Nevada State Trooper

Also by Steve Raabe

Patrolling the Heart of the West

Patrolling
the
Heart
of the
Silver State

More True Tales from a Nevada State Trooper

Steve Raabe

LATAH
BOOKS

Events, conversations, and locations were recreated from the author's memory of them. In some instances, the names and details of individuals and places have been altered to protect anonymity.

Book and cover design by Kevin Breen

Cover image derived from Adobe Stock photos

ISBN: 978-1-957607-30-6

Cataloging-in-Publication Data is available upon request

Manufactured in the United States of America

Published by
Latah Books, Spokane, Washington
www.latahbooks.com

The author may be contacted at snowraabe@gmail.com

Praise for *Patrolling the Heart of the Silver State*

"*Patrolling the Heart of the Silver State* is an enduring salutation to a way of life that cannot be viewed as a job, a career, or even a profession. It is a calling, and one has to hear that call to truly understand what such a life entails. Though I have never met Steve Raabe personally, I know his kind. We are blessed to have them among us."
—Ben H. English, author of *Black and White: Tales of the Texas Highway Patrol*

"A great continuation into the life of a Nevada Highway Patrolman and his journey through the ranks. From operations in the field to working administration, there's never a dull moment. What a wonderful tribute to a career that many will never truly understand but will appreciate and respect."
—Tony Almaraz, former chief of the Nevada Highway Patrol

"Steve Raabe was a career highway patrolman who took his job very seriously, and himself much less so. This is a wonderful, humorous and at times poignant look back on a career well served."
—Mike Alger, KTVN TV Chief Meteorologist, Reno, Nevada and author of *Snow Storm*

Praise for *Patrolling the Heart of the West,* Raabe's original collection of stories

"Though many of his true tales take tragic and terrifying turns, Raabe's grace, compassion and good cheer, along with a wicked sense of humor, shine through..."
—*Las Vegas Review-Journal*

"*Patrolling the Heart of the West* can easily be digested in short spurts, but it's possible that when you start reading this book that it will be impossible to put down."
—*Sparks Tribune*

"Told with great humor and compassion, Raabe's tales show us the heart behind the badge."
—Michael Gurian, *NY Times* bestselling author of *The Wonder of Boys*

"Whether you have an interest in law enforcement, are a fan of all things Nevadan, or just want to enjoy a good book that you won't want to put down once you start reading it, you'll find *Patrolling the Heart of the West* to be a memorable read. Highly recommended."

—Excerpt from *Readers' Favorite*, review by Kimberlee J Benart

"*Patrolling the Heart of the West* is a thoroughly entertaining and enlightening read. With a style reminiscent of the war stories exchanged during a law-enforcement family barbecue, Raabe's skill as a storyteller is evident as he imparts his wisdom and experience with a unique sense of humor, candor, and insightfulness."

—Andy Brown, author of *Warnings Unheeded: Twin Tragedies at Fairchild Air Force Base*

"*Patrolling the Heart of the West* is a quick, entertaining and informative glimpse into an important, sometimes dangerous career spent in a unique, little understood corner of the country."

—Ed Pearce, Senior Reporter, KOLO-TV Reno

"Raabe tells his experiences with excellent accuracy, grace and wit. I couldn't put the book down!"

—Colonel Michael Hood, Nevada Highway Patrol

"Perhaps the most endearing police memoir yet written. As a son and brother of cops, I admire the humanity Raabe brings to each of these stories."   —Jon Gosch, author of *Deep Fire Rise*

"Raabe's stories reflect 'the good, the bad and the ugly' aspects of patrolling our highways. *Patrolling the Heart of the West* will bring a new appreciation for the unique role and responsibilities of state troopers, especially those who work in rural or remote areas."

—G Paul Corbin, criminal justice professor and former chief of the Nevada Highway Patrol

Dedication

This book is dedicated to my oldest son, Nevada State Police Sergeant Timothy Lee Raabe, and his Belgian Malinois K-9 partner and best friend, Gripper Raabe. Tim and Gripper (now deceased) worked together for many years and became one of the very best K-9 drug teams to ever work in the state of Nevada. Their reputation for excellence and success was well-known, and in addition to their daily duties working the highways, they were called upon often to assist federal, state, and local agencies in the pursuit of illegal drugs and drug traffickers throughout northern Nevada.

Tim has almost twenty years on the job and has excelled in every endeavor he has undertaken—patrolman, detective, field-training officer, sergeant, K-9 handler, and defensive tactics expert certifying instructors. The state of Nevada is lucky to have him as a trooper, and I am lucky to have him as son. A father could not be prouder.

Contents

Foreword

I would like to begin by saying thank you to all who purchased, read, shared, and promoted my first book, *Patrolling the Heart of the West: True Tales of a Nevada State Trooper*. From book signings and sales at local libraries, book retailers, and Costco stores to its persistent placement among Amazon's top-ranking Law Enforcement Biographies for the last five years, its success has been exciting, fun, unbelievable, and humbling—and I owe it all to you.

It is a strange time for police and police agencies across our nation, as many citizens have been told by a few that law enforcement officers are not to be trusted and are the enemy. Because of this trend, some might think it an odd time to write and publish a sequel to my first book, but I think it an ideal time, as so many people could use a better understanding of the job of law enforcement and the people who perform these tasks daily. I was amazed and pleased at the number of comments from readers who claimed to have a much better understanding of a highway patrolman's job after reading my book.

Most Americans have gained what little actual knowledge they have of police work from a lifetime of television and movies, and like most everything produced in Hollywood, it is far from the truth. On television, the FBI waltzes in and takes over any case they want to from local agencies, officers are shot at weekly, and many police officers take bribes and abuse innocent citizens. But in real life, these scenarios are the exceptions, not the rule.

While being shot is a very real possibility, on average only 245 out of 800,000 officers in America are shot each year, 42 of which are fatal. I spent a good portion of my life as a state trooper and only knew a handful of officers who were involved in shootings, including my very lucky son, Nevada State Police Sergeant Tim Raabe, whose very close call with death is included in this book.

American police hunting down and harming innocent people is one of the most ridiculous, non-proven rumors spread in my lifetime. As a retired state trooper, I never once started my day with the intention of hurting anyone, nor can I recall one coworker or associate over an entire career who did. Most of us went to work each day expecting to help others and save lives one way or another. Citizens know of officers saving the lives of severely injured people by controlling bleeding, treating for shock, opening airways, administering CPR, or some other action like pulling them out of a burning car or house, but few think about the number of lives saved through the everyday enforcement of traffic and criminal laws. Every dangerous driver cited, every DUI driver arrested, every violent criminal caught, and every violent domestic situation dealt with is a potential life saved.

As a whole, America's law enforcement officers today, regardless of the agency they work for, are better educated, selected, and trained than at any other time in our nation's history, and I would gladly put them up against any other police officers in the world. Except for a handful of bad apples that bring discredit to the noble profession, every other law enforcement officer deserves your respect and support.

This book, like my first one, is filled with stories of the day-to-day experiences common to the job of being a state trooper in the vast American West. These are the rest of the stories from my career, and I have included a few stories of incidents experienced by a couple of state trooper friends and my son. I truly hope you enjoy reading them, and once again, thank you for your interest.

One final note: My identification number changed three times over my career, from #7376 to #6144 to #3067.

Sincerely,

Steven E. Raabe
Nevada Highway Patrol ID #3067 (retired)

Tell Him, Stupid

When I began my career as a state trooper in the fall of 1980, I was assigned as a cadet to Nevada Highway Patrol Academy, Class #16. At the time, all troopers in our state were required to become certified Emergency Medical Technicians (EMTs). While most of the existing troopers completed this extensive 120 hours of training over an extended period of time, those of us in an academy setting had three weeks to complete it.

Looking back years later, the training and knowledge were invaluable, but the application was not practical. Other than attending to what are called the ABCs (Airway, Breathing, and Circulation) of treatment, there was very little we could do without medical equipment, which our employer didn't furnish. In addition to 120 hours of classroom training, we were required to spend eight hours in an emergency room or riding an ambulance.

A good friend of mine arrived one morning at Washoe Medical Center (now known as Renown) to start his eight-hour shift when a paramedic assigned to the local air ambulance asked if he wanted to spend his required time riding in a helicopter. Who in their right mind would say no? I wasn't quite so lucky.

I was assigned to spend my eight-hour shift in the Washoe Medical Center emergency room. I arrived one Saturday morning raring to go and excited, only to be met by a very impatient and angry head nurse. She was obviously not interested in my required training, and after having difficulty obtaining a patient's blood pressure, she told me to

1

leave and get more practice before I returned. My academy lieutenant was not happy with my result and the fact that the head nurse sent me home, so all emergency room training was moved to St. Mary's Hospital in Reno.

I arrived at St. Mary's the next Saturday morning, and after working in the emergency room for a while, I was outfitted with a white lab coat and sent to a small room that had a sign reading, "Triage." I was the first contact for non-life-threatening illnesses and injuries. This is where I met an injured eight-year-old boy and his father. I took a quick break and returned to find the two of them seated in my triage room. The boy was rocking back and forth in the chair and crying. He was squeezing the index finger of his left hand in his right fist and was in a considerable amount of pain. Dad sat there with a disgusted look on his face and showed little sympathy.

I greeted them and, as required, took the boy's temperature and blood pressure.

"What happened to you, young man?" I asked.

Before the boy could answer, Dad reached up, slapped his son in the back of the head, and said, "Tell him, stupid. Tell him what you did!"

I immediately felt sorry for the little guy, but when the boy related the story of his injured finger to me, I could hardly fault Dad for his actions.

Around the corner from St. Mary's is the Circus Circus Hotel and Casino. In addition to gambling, the casino is famous for ongoing circus acts, a giant arcade, and carnival-style games for children.

The carnival game where this young boy received his injury was called "Shooting Stars." A white paper target with a small red star in the center is hung up in the carnival-style shooting range. The player fires a mounted BB machine gun at the red star, and if the star is completely shot out, they win.

This boy was shooting at the star and stopped after firing numerous BBs. Then, in order to see if he had any BBs left to shoot, he placed his left index finger over the end of the barrel, pulled the trigger, and promptly and painfully filled the end of his fingertip with BBs.

I looked at the injury and could see that the BBs had passed through the fleshy part of his finger and lodged themselves directly under his fingernail. You can bet this hurt like hell.

Perhaps Dad was negligent in his fatherly duties. Maybe the boy's actions were so quick, Dad couldn't stop him. But after the deed was done, Dad's job was to make sure this kid never did anything like it again. That is where the son's memory of a slap in the back of the head might be useful in the future, although filling his fingertip with BBs might have sufficed.

Imagine My Surprise

Horses were my main source of transportation as a boy. My mother, Charlotte, loved to ride, and my great-grandmother, Esther Gibbs Pawson, whom I adored, was one of the very first rodeo cowgirls in the west, claiming the title of World Champion Relay Rider at the Frontier Days Rodeo in Cheyenne, Wyoming in 1906. I guess my love of horses wasn't a choice, but when I was thirteen years of age, my parents divorced, and owning horses was no longer included in the meager family budget.

In May of 1975, I was very busy going to school at Carson High, working part-time for the state, and traveling every weekend to a different town to compete in my last year of high school rodeo. No longer owning a horse meant I had to compete in rodeo events where I could ride someone else's horse (and bulls). So, every Friday after school, my buddies and I would head out in someone's car with our rodeo gear, snacks, very little money, and no parents. I mention no parents because young men at that age really should have been accompanied by at least one. Without fully developed brains, young men are quite good at making stupid decisions, and believe me we were not exceptions to the rule.

The next scheduled high school rodeo was at Battle Mountain, Nevada, and it was my turn to drive. My old car had recently died, and I needed something to drive, so I called my good friend Kurt Henning's father, Howie, who owned a Ford dealership in the town of

Fallon where I grew up. Mr. Henning and his wife Pat were wonderful people. They took me deer hunting, fed me from time to time, and treated me very well. When I asked Mr. Henning about buying a used car, he said, "I have a 1967 Chevy Impala for five hundred dollars that you might like. Come pick it up, drive it around, and if you like it, I will get you the paperwork."

When Friday afternoon arrived, four of us dumb cowboys jumped in my new car with no license plates and no paperwork showing it was mine and headed off to the town of Battle Mountain 250 miles away. Now, if you think driving halfway across the state of Nevada in a used car with no license plates was a bad idea, just to be extra stupid we added a case of beer to the mix.

The first law enforcement encounter of the evening was with a Lyon County deputy near the little town of Silver Springs who pulled us over for having no license plates. I explained the entire story of how I had acquired the car (the beer safely stowed away in the trunk), and we were turned loose with a warning.

The second encounter occurred on I-80 just outside of the town of Winnemucca when a Nevada State trooper pulled me over for having no license plates. Again, I explained my story.

This time, the trooper was not nearly as forgiving as the deputy, saying, "You can't be driving around without license plates or documentation showing that this car belongs to you. Where are you four young men headed to?"

"We're members of the Carson High School rodeo team," I said. "We're headed to Battle Mountain to compete in the rodeo this weekend."

"You know, I could impound this car right now for no registration and have it towed off. If I did so, where would that leave you?"

"Well, sir," I said, "I guess it would leave us walking to Battle

Mountain with bull ropes, bareback riggings, and what little clothes we brought with us."

About that time, the nosy trooper, who was looking all over with his flashlight, happened to spot a beer can. It—along with several others—had previously made the trip from the trunk to the backseat.

"Well, this night just keeps on getting better and better," he said. "Everybody out of the car. Where is the rest of the beer that you are all too young to have?"

We *yes sir'd* and *no sir'd* this poor trooper to death as we produced every can in a matter of seconds.

"Alright," he said. "Pull the tabs on each can and pour them out."

After pouring out all the beer, we received a world-class butt chewing and were turned loose. I have always joked that the Nevada Highway Patrol hired me because they couldn't catch me, but it certainly wasn't true that night.

Fast forward five years and seven months to December 8th, 1980. I was twenty-three years old and had just graduated from the Nevada Highway Patrol Academy three days prior. At exactly 8:00 a.m., I walked into my new duty station in Winnemucca to meet my Field Training Officer, Trooper George McIntosh. Imagine my surprise when he turned out to be the very same trooper who had chewed me out and owed me a case of beer. Trooper McIntosh didn't recognize me from our chance encounter, and I didn't bring it up until I was out of training and working on my own.

There were many young men from my generation who poured alcohol into the thirsty Nevada desert, but those days are gone. In today's litigious society, any law enforcement officer who failed to arrest juveniles found with alcohol would be sued to high heaven if anything happened to the kids afterwards.

Trooper George McIntosh was one of the finest state troopers I ever worked with. We became good friends, and we still keep in touch with one another. Over the years, George has returned my beer one can at a time, and I think I eventually came out ahead.

Our Sergeant, Our Mentor, Our Friend

Tuesday, December 9, 1980 was my second day on the job as a Nevada State trooper. My academy classmate, Doug Darlington, and I had recently moved our young families to our assigned duty station of Winnemucca, and both of us were excited. Our new sergeant Michael Curti's regular days off were Sunday and Monday, so the first order of business at 8:00 a.m. on this cold Tuesday morning was to meet with him at the office.

Sergeant Curti had taught a four-hour class on Nevada History and Geography at our academy and had contacted each of us a couple of times to help us find housing, but other than that we knew little about him. All we knew was that after a very long, stressful academy environment, sergeants were close to God on the important list.

The highway patrol Winnemucca District covered over 22,000 square miles, which is twice the size of the state of Massachusetts. It included three large counties, each with several small towns, and three Native American reservations. Sergeant Curti welcomed us to our new duty station and then proceeded to fill our heads with a wealth of information concerning our new district, including the different law enforcement agencies, district attorneys' offices, hospitals, ambulance corps, and tow companies we would be working with, as well as several different Nevada Department of Transportation offices available to us and how to obtain fuel at each.

The numerous courts we had to deal with were a topic of their own. The three counties in our district were made up of different small townships, each with their own judges, court appearance dates, addresses, various bail amounts set by each judge, and unique instructions for how to contact them day or night to request a warrant.

Our sergeant covered numerous roadways and state highways that we were responsible for and the beat number of each for documentation of citations and accidents and other pertinent information. The meeting continued, and luckily, we were both supplied with a binder containing most of the information that had just been covered.

Toward the end of the meeting, Sergeant Curti discussed the human aspects of our area: which local cops were good to work with, which ones to stay away from, which residents had threatened officers, which were known to carry firearms, and which were most likely to fight if confronted. This was followed by very important information about where to take coffee breaks and which restaurants served the best meals.

Finally, Sergeant Curti addressed the last topic of the day and said, "As discussed earlier, State Route 140 connects northwestern Nevada to southern Oregon. It intersects US 95 thirty-three miles north of Winnemucca and proceeds one hundred and ten miles farther west to the Oregon state line. It is a very sparsely populated area. At mile marker 65, there is a small bar, restaurant, and motel called Denio Junction. It is owned by Lee and Nancy Greenstreet who are wonderful people who take great care of us anytime we are out there. Quite often, your highway patrol radio will not work that far out, and you can count on them to lend a hand when needed."

Sergeant Curti paused for effect before continuing. "The Greenstreets make the one-hundred-mile trip to Winnemucca at least once, sometimes twice a week for supplies. They do not have a refrigerated vehicle to transport perishables like vegetables, meat, and ice cream. In winter months it is not a problem, but crossing one hundred miles of hot desert in the summertime is. So, this is the rule:

If the Greenstreets are on their way to town or it is winter, they are expected to drive the speed limit. If they are on their way home in warm weather loaded with supplies, they are not to be messed with."

I learned during my career that supervising new state troopers can be a challenge. They are fresh out of school, excited about their new jobs, have an unbelievable amount of influence and power over others' lives, and lack the common sense and discretion that most develop with time, experience, and under the guidance of a capable sergeant, which I believe is the most critically important position in any law enforcement agency. Sergeant Mike Curti was a teacher, mentor, and friend. I and my fellow Winnemucca District troopers were quite lucky to have him. Therefore, I could not miss the opportunity to include a few Mike Curti stories in my book.

Prior to being promoted to sergeant in Winnemucca, Mike Curti was a trooper in the Las Vegas District. One day, while on patrol on US 95 south of Las Vegas, Trooper Curti was advised by dispatch to look for the driver of a red sports car traveling northbound. It was reported that the driver of the red sports car pulled up beside the driver of a white four-door sedan and motioned for him to pull over and stop. The driver of the white car pulled over, and when he stepped out, the driver of the red sports car walked up to him and punched him square in the nose. The victim with the sore nose demanded that the driver of the red car be located and charged with assault and battery.

Within minutes, Mike found the red sports car, pulled it over, and asked the driver, "Did you flag down the driver of a white sedan and punch him in the nose?"

"Yes, I did," said the driver. "And if I see the dirty rat again, I will give him another one!"

"Why did you do it?" Mike asked.

"I make this trip often," said the man. "Occasionally, I see the remains of desert tortoises that were killed crossing the highway.

Today, I was right behind that guy when he ran over a desert tortoise on purpose."

"Are you sure it wasn't an accident?" Mike asked.

"It was not an accident. The desert tortoise was on the very edge of the pavement, and the guy had to drive out of his lane to hit it."

Mike told him, "The man that you punched wants to sign a criminal complaint against you for battery, and we are going to go meet with him. Get in your car and follow me. Once we get there, I want you to remain inside your vehicle."

Mike met with the driver of the white car and asked him if he'd run over a desert tortoise on purpose.

"Maybe," stated the driver. "But even if I did, that does not give that guy the right to punch me in the nose. I want him arrested!"

"I can do that," Mike stated. "But if you press charges against this man for punching you in the nose, I will have to charge you with killing an endangered and protected species. It is a federal crime to kill a desert tortoise and it carries a big fine and possible jail time."

Mike told me this story on a long road trip we were taking and summed it up by saying, "The day ended perfectly. The tortoise killer received a well-deserved punch in the nose and decided not to press charges. The puncher received a stern warning against taking such actions in the future. And I didn't have to spend the rest of the shift writing arrest reports."

Another day, three of my fellow troopers and I were scheduled to attend a class at the Winnemucca Police Department at 8:00 a.m. The four of us met at the highway patrol office about 7:30 a.m. and were speaking with Sergeant Curti when dispatch advised us of a gas skip in the small town of McDermitt on US 95, seventy-four miles north of Winnemucca. A gray four-door sedan occupied by two white males filled up with gas at the McDermitt Chevron station and left without paying. The car was last seen heading south on US 95 toward Winnemucca.

Even though we were scheduled to attend class, Trooper Dave Black and I were assigned to day shift that month, so we grabbed our gear and started for our patrol cars.

Sergeant Curti stopped us and said, "All of you go to class. I will take this one."

Any officer or trooper who has dealt with gas skips knows that fueling up and leaving without paying is occasionally an honest mistake, but most often it is an intentional act perpetrated by criminals.

"Sarge, are you sure you don't want any help?" I asked. "You know darn well this gas skip is probably going to be bad guys or a stolen car or both!"

"Maybe," he said. "But go to class, and I will call you guys if I need you."

Sergeant Curti got into his patrol car and headed north while the four of us walked across the street to the police department.

We were about a half hour into the class when the secretary from the police department opened the classroom door and stated, "Sergeant Curti needs his troops. He's in pursuit of two suspects wanted in Idaho for a strong-armed robbery. He is southbound on US 95, just passing State Route 290."

The four of us jumped up from our desks, ran across the street to our individual patrol cars, and took off to the north. We listened to the radio with excitement as our experienced sergeant, traveling more than one hundred miles per hour, calmly provided updates on the current location of the pursuit. About five miles north of Winnemucca, the four of us positioned our patrol cars across US 95, leaving an escape route to the right side of the roadway should the crooks choose not to stop. All four of us were armed with 12-gauge shotguns and took up positions behind our cars.

US 95 is a two-lane, bi-directional highway, and the area we chose to block off had narrow shoulders and steep drop-offs on both sides of the highway. If the two crooks chose not to stop and tried to take the only opening of escape that we left them, it would have likely ended in a crash.

One positive aspect of working in rural Nevada is that there are few paved highways or roads, making it very difficult for non-residents unfamiliar with the area to take another route. As the pursuit approached our roadblock, the robbers saw more flashing lights in one place than anyone in the Nevada desert had seen in a long time. Realizing that they were outnumbered with nowhere to run, they stopped their car and gave up. Bingo! It turned out that these two yoyos had robbed an elderly lady of her purse and while doing so had beaten her so badly that she had to be admitted to a Boise hospital.

Not long after this event, Sergeant Curti and I were working early one Saturday morning when a call came in to assist a Humboldt County deputy with an empty stolen car parked in front of the 49er Truck Stop on I-80 west of Winnemucca. Both Sergeant Curti and I arrived about the same time and met with Humboldt County Deputy Matt Paszek at the commercial fuel pumps behind the main building.

Deputy Paszek, who years later became Trooper Paszek, was very new to police work and was quite excited that he had spotted his first stolen car thought to be in the possession of a wanted fugitive. Deputy Paszek was eager to find and arrest the culprit, but we had no idea what the suspect looked like or if he was still anywhere in the vicinity, so he looked to Sergeant Curti for direction.

Deputy Paszek asked, "Hey, Sarge, what do you think we ought to do?"

Sarge looked at him and said, "It's seven-thirty in the morning. I say we go inside and have breakfast."

Deputy Paszek was shocked by my wise sergeant's response.

"Breakfast?" he asked. "Are you kidding?"

"No, Deputy Paszek. It is definitely time for breakfast," said Sarge. "We are going to drive our three patrol cars around to the front and park in the same area as the stolen car. Then we are going to walk into the restaurant, sit at a booth with a view of the stolen car, and order breakfast. If the bad guy is still here and takes off in the car, we will be right behind him.

There were a couple of dozen truck drivers and patrons in the restaurant, so we ordered our breakfast. Halfway through our meal, we saw a man get up from a booth and pay his bill. Obviously not suspecting that we knew anything about him, he walked outside, climbed into the stolen car, and drove off.

The three of us walked out to our patrol cars and watched from a distance as the suspect pulled onto I-80 headed west. After giving him a little head start, we proceeded westbound and caught up to him a couple miles down the road. After seeing three patrol cars in his rearview mirror lit up like Christmas trees, the suspect pulled over and was taken into custody without incident. Deputy Matt Paszek had his first felony arrest, and the sarge and I had a good laugh.

Mike Curti loved being a highway patrol sergeant, loved the town of Winnemucca and its citizens, and took great care of the young troopers he supervised. He led by example, worked hard, took his share of callouts in the middle of the night, and demonstrated professionalism, compassion, and respect for everyone, even those he arrested. He never asked anything of his troopers that he would not do himself. He corrected us when we made mistakes and had our backs when we were right. He taught all of us how to be top-notch state troopers and what it took to be good supervisors and commanders as most of us moved up in rank during our careers. We were so fortunate to have this man as our sergeant, our mentor, and our friend.

Mike retired in 1985, and he and wife Mary Lou opened a restaurant in downtown Winnemucca. Mike's Restaurante and Cantina became our new hangout, and my wife Janelle and I held our wedding in the Curtis's front yard in 1987. Mike and Mary Lou, tired of cold Nevada winters, became snowbirds and bought a place in Yuma, Arizona in 1999. When I retired from the highway patrol in 2001, Janelle and I bought a house about a mile away from Mike and Mary Lou's Yuma house, and the four of us spent many wonderful winters together until Mike's health prevented him from traveling.

My first book, *Patrolling the Heart of the West*, in which Sergeant Michael Curti was mentioned numerous times, was being published as he was coming close to the end of his life. The sadness of saying goodbye to someone you love is always difficult, but seeing Mike smile in the hospital as I read my entire book to him aloud helped offset the pain.

When Sergeant Mike Curti passed away at the age of eighty-six, more than two dozen of Mike's troops attended his services at the Catholic Church in Winnemucca, where he was given one heck of a sendoff to Heaven by those who loved him. Rest in peace, #5072. You were loved and respected by many!

Hippity Hoppity

Other than talking to my friends on cheap walkie-talkies as a child, I had never been on either end of a radio until my second actual day at work as a trooper. Even during months of training at an academy, where every vehicle we rode in had radios, cadets didn't use them.

At 7:45 a.m. on my second day of work, Trooper McIntosh, driving a bright, shiny, blue-and-silver patrol car, pulled up in front of the little travel trailer I had crammed my family into after graduating from the academy in Reno three days prior.

I opened the door and sat down in the warm patrol car, and the first thing Trooper George McIntosh said to me was, "You need to check on-duty."

"How exactly do I do that?" I asked.

"Well, you pick up the radio mic, push the button, give them your ID number, and tell them you're at work."

That may seem like a simple process, but for the first time there was nothing easy about it. I remember looking at the mic hanging on its clip on the metal radio rack and feeling very awkward. I had spent months learning how to use firearms, night sticks, self-defense, and studied everything from riot and mob control to disarming assailants. Now, the supposedly simple act of talking on a police radio to a person on the other end had me intimidated.

"Are you going to check on-duty or just look at it?" George asked.

I picked up the mic, looked at my FTO, and asked, "Ok, what exactly do I say?"

"You say, 'Elko, 7376,' wait for them to answer you by saying your number, then you say, '10-41,' which means 'I am on duty!'" he said with a roll of his eyes and a shake of his head.

I did as he directed, but the clumsy, awkward feeling took days to disappear. Before I knew it, talking on the police radio was as natural as walking and breathing. Over the years, there were times when I was ecstatic to have one, and other times when I wished I didn't have one at all.

*

2:30 a.m. Easter Sunday, 1981, I was responding to a commercial vehicle accident on State Route 140. The highway began thirty-three miles north of Winnemucca at a junction with US 95 and ran for another 110 miles to the Oregon state line. I had only been about one hundred miles out State Route 140 in the few short months of my career, and I was somewhere beyond that when Elko dispatch called and requested my 10-20 (location).

I picked up the radio mic and said, "Elko, I have no idea where I am. It's snowing like crazy, and I'm way the heck out here, but I can't tell you where. When I pass the next highway mile marker, if I can see it, I will let you know."

The next thing I heard was my dispatcher singing, "Here comes Peter Cottontail, hopping down the bunny trail."

I smiled, picked up the mic, and finished it, "Hippity, hoppity, Easter's on its way!"

Her timing was perfect. I'm sure we were the only two working in that large northern portion of Nevada at that time, and it made me feel a lot better knowing that I wasn't completely alone.

*

Hitchhiking is against the law in Nevada, but the law is seldom enforced. Since it is against the law, troopers had the legal right to question hitchhikers, see their ID, and check them for warrants. I have arrested many wanted criminals hitchhiking across Nevada, but the vast majority checked out fine and were allowed to continue.

One fine spring morning, I came upon a Native American male, hitchhiking eastbound on I-80, about four miles east of Winnemucca. I advised dispatch I would be out with an IMA (Indian Male Adult) and gave her my location. I stopped my patrol car and approached the man. My spiel was the same every time I contacted a hitchhiker. I would advise them that hitchhiking in our state was illegal, but we seldom bothered anyone as long as they didn't cause any problems for the motoring public. The man was dressed in blue jeans and a denim shirt, had some eagle feathers in his hat, and wore turquoise rings and bracelets. I asked for the man's identification, which he promptly located in his wallet and handed to me. I obtained the man's Social Security Number and told him to hang tight and I would be right back.

I returned to my car and read the Native American man's driver's license. I needed to contact dispatch by radio and give her his name, date of birth, and social security number so she could check for wants and warrants nationwide and locally. I really wasn't looking forward to this wants check, but I didn't have a choice.

"Elko, 6144."

"6144."

"10-29 (check for wants and warrants), IMA, first name Harry, last name Beaver."

"10-4, 6144. Is first name common spelling?" my female dispatcher asked with a chuckle.

Was my dispatcher implying that Harry could be spelled another way?

"10-4, Elko. Common spelling on my subject's first name!" Now I was chuckling.

A minute or two passed, and dispatch called back.

"6144, Elko." I could tell right away that it wasn't just my dispatcher

18

laughing; it was the entire dispatch center.

"6144, go ahead."

"6144 (amidst continual laughing and snorting), your subject, Harry Beaver, has no wants, no warrants, negative NCIC (National Crime Information Center), negative CJIS (Criminal Justice Information System)."

At this point, I was barely able to talk, as laughter is quite contagious. "10-4, Elko."

Anyway, Mr. Harry Beaver was allowed to continue on his way, and I had another day working the highway that I would never forget.

*

While there were certainly some funny days on the radio, there were also radio days that were not funny and at times embarrassing. In the early 80s, our high-band police radio was prone to a condition called skip. Skip occurs when radio waves are reflected back to earth by the ionosphere. This caused some very unexpected, long-distance communication interference on the radio.

In these days, we had no handheld radios, so every time we left our patrol cars we would turn on an outside radio speaker so we could hear radio traffic and dispatch, should they call. The problem with broadcasting the radio traffic was that everyone in the car you just stopped could hear it as well, which could be detrimental to the trooper's welfare. One of our troopers was shot one night on the Strip in Las Vegas when dispatch announced that the vehicle the trooper was out with had been reported sold. The vehicle had actually been stolen. The thought was that when the bad guy heard dispatch say sold over the speaker, he might have mistaken it for stole because immediately afterward he came out of the car shooting. No one ever knew for sure if the man mistook the word sold for stole because after putting one bullet in the trooper's stomach, the trooper put six .357 Magnum bullets in the man before he hit the ground dead. The trooper, Dan

Hammack, recovered from his wounds and went on to become the best operational command officer I ever worked for.

Quite often, we would hear police traffic from far away. The Culpeper, Virginia Police Department was on our same frequency and came across our radio in the middle of the Nevada desert as if they were right next door. Sometimes, everyone in the vehicles we were stopping would hear police radio traffic with deep southern accents. Other times, you never knew where the skip was coming from or what you would hear.

One morning, I made a traffic stop on a car with three occupants. I had completed the citation, approached the vehicle, and was explaining the citation to the driver when radio skip came over my loudspeaker. Unfortunately, it wasn't police traffic from Culpeper. It was skip I had never heard before, and it went like this:

"Yogi Bear to Boo-Boo, Yogi Bear to Boo-Boo!"

"Go ahead, Yogi."

"Did you get the dumpster behind Denny's?"

"10-4, Yogi. I picked it up a while ago."

It turned out this radio traffic that sounded so professional I wanted to crawl under my patrol car and disappear was a garbage company in Boise, Idaho. With the installation of new radio equipment in the mid-80s, skip vanished from our lives, but it wasn't missed.

*

Right behind Alaska, Nevada is the second-most mountainous state in America, having over 314 individual mountain ranges with forty peaks reaching well over 10,000 ft. in elevation. Our high-band radio system, which covered the seventh-largest state, was comprised of radio repeaters on the tallest mountaintops, strategically selected to provide the best coverage along Nevada's remote highways. Each of these mountaintops received and relayed radio traffic between dispatch and us. Each radio repeater was named and labeled in the dispatch center for the mountaintop it was located on, like Maggie Peak,

Toulon Peak, and Winnemucca Mountain, which was the repeater that relayed the majority of my radio traffic to and from dispatch. So our dispatchers could see where in our giant state a radio call was coming from by which mountaintop repeater it utilized.

Another embarrassing incident occurred very early one summer morning while I was working the 6:00 p.m. to 2:00 a.m. shift. At about 1:00 a.m., with one hour to go, I decided to pull off the highway and watch traffic for a while. I took an off-ramp, drove up a remote canyon about a quarter of a mile, turned out the lights with a good view of the interstate, and sat. The truckers always kept perfect track of us and relayed our location to each other on their CB radios. We couldn't get away from them, and they were damn hard to catch, but when we flat out disappeared, it drove them crazy.

So there I was, all alone, in the dark, kicked back, watching traffic, listening to the police radio, the CB radio, and some tunes. I always had tunes on in the patrol car. I was a great singer as long as I was alone in a car or behind a curtain in the shower, so while I was parked there I belted out a few songs. After about fifteen minutes of not seeing anyone worthy of chasing, I decided to get back on the road. As soon as I sat up straight and put my car in drive, my radio went off.

"6144, Elko."

"6144."

"Was that you singing the last fifteen minutes, or did you hear that concert coming off Winnemucca Mountain as well?"

Oh crap! Apparently, when I was kicked back in my car, I'd rested my right knee against my radio mic, sitting there for fifteen minutes singing to dispatch and God knows how many other people that monitored our radio traffic. If there were a hole big enough to crawl into and disappear, I would have.

"Elko, 6144. Sorry about that!"

"6144, it's okay. It was just you and me and the entire northern portion of the state!" (Chuckle, chuckle.)

A Valuable Lesson Learned

My academy training was followed by twelve weeks of field training where every minute of every day was spent working with an experienced trooper in our new duty stations. These specially trained troopers taught us how to be self-sufficient, how to stay alive, and how to perform our daily tasks. They coached, observed, corrected, rated, graded, and documented everything we did daily, whether we did it well or needed improvement. It was a stressful time, but necessary to ensure the success and welfare of new troopers, especially those of us assigned to rural Nevada where we always worked alone and backup or support from another officer in a timely manner was non-existent. As much as these training officers prepared us to work on our own, they couldn't predict everything that we would experience, so the school of hard knocks took over.

It is both exciting and ominous to be turned loose as a new trooper. After six months of being on edge in a stressful academy environment and the field-training period, one can finally take a relaxed, non-observed, non-graded breath. However, the feeling of freedom is clouded by the inevitable call to a very serious accident or situation. Every time dispatch calls your number on the radio, your heart flutters just a little, hoping it is nothing serious. We were well-trained and prepared, but the only way to cure the "will I do it right" feeling is experience.

It was February 28, 1981, 10:30 a.m. on a beautiful Saturday morning, and it was my second day of working on my own. As a matter of fact, I was the only trooper scheduled to work that morning for a hundred miles in either direction. I guess my new boss, Sergeant Mike Curti, had more faith in my abilities than I did.

I was about thirty-five miles west of Winnemucca on I-80 when I observed a large four-door Cadillac eastbound at a high rate of speed. Not being radar-certified, my only option was to get behind the vehicle and pace it by matching its speed. I got as close as possible without being seen and followed the violator closely, matching their speed, then slowing down a couple of miles per hour. If the distance between our vehicles increased, I could issue a citation for the lower speed. I paced the vehicle in excess of 85 mph in a 55-mph zone.

I caught up to the vehicle and pulled it over. It was occupied by four adult males who appeared to be in their forties. The driver climbed out, met me at the rear of his car, and handed me his driver's license and registration. His name was Arvil Pope, and he was quite the jokester. I advised Mr. Pope that I had checked his speed at more than 85 mph, and he proceeded to tell me that I was crazy. I asked him why he was speeding, and he told me that he and his friends were headed to Simone's (one of four legal brothels in Winnemucca), and their wives were chasing them. All the windows in the Cadillac were rolled down, and his buddies who were listening to the conversation were laughing, thinking him to be quite the comedian. Mr. Pope continued fast-talking and joking around, and when I finally got a chance to get a few words in, I advised him that I would be issuing him a citation for speeding.

I returned to my patrol car and wrote out Mr. Pope's citation. Since the Cadillac was filled with an audience that Mr. Pope enjoyed entertaining, I asked him to come back to my vehicle where I would explain his options to him. Mr. Pope continued talking, joking around, and interrupting me, so it took a few extra minutes to complete my task. The options were the same for everybody. Either to appear in court at the date and time specified on the citation, or if that date was not convenient, he could contact the court and reschedule an appearance date, or he could send in the bail (fine) amount of $65 as indicated on the citation to the justice court prior to his appearance date.

Finally, I advised Mr. Pope that I needed his signature at the bottom of the citation. It is not an admission of guilt but simply a promise to appear in court or take care of the citation as instructed.

Mr. Pope looked at me and said, "I don't think I want to sign it!"

"Mr. Pope," I said, "not signing the citation is not an option. If you refuse to sign the citation, I must arrest you and take you to jail. I am asking you again to please sign the citation."

"No, I don't think I am going to sign it."

A violator not signing a citation was certainly discussed in training, but it was a first for me. I really didn't want to arrest Mr. Pope on my second day, so I tried two more times.

"Mr. Pope," I pleaded again, "if you don't sign the citation, I have to arrest you, and I sure don't want to have to take you to jail today!"

"Well, I guess you will have to arrest me then."

I placed my ticket book on the hood of the car and asked Mr. Pope to turn around and place his hands behind his back.

Then the big jokester suddenly returned. Laughing, smiling, and fast-talking again, Mr. Pope said, "Ha-ha, I am just kidding with you. Of course, I am going to sign it."

I allowed Mr. Pope to sign the citation, and we parted company.

My day was over at 2:00 p.m., and I went home. About 9:00 p.m. that night, my phone rang. It was one of my training officers, Trooper Rick Bradley. Trooper Bradley asked me if I had stopped a man by the name of Arvil Pope for speeding earlier in the day. I told him that I had cited Mr. Pope and that he had given me some trouble not wanting to sign the citation.

Trooper Bradley asked, "Did you take sixty-five dollars in cash from Mr. Pope for the speeding violation?"

I had been on my own for two whole days, and none of my coworkers knew me that well, so I was quite upset and told Trooper Bradley, "No, I did not!"

"Well, he claims that you took the money."

"Well, I didn't," I said. "Nor would I ever! How on earth did you get this information? Did Mr. Pope come into the highway patrol office?"

"No, I stopped him with three of his buddies for speeding this evening, and he told me this story on his way to jail."

"Why did you arrest him?" I asked.

"He told me that he wouldn't sign the citation."

"He told me the same thing!"

"How many times did you ask him to sign?" Trooper Bradley asked.

"Four," I said. "How many times did you ask him to sign?"

"Once."

"Did he start joking around and tell you that he was just kidding and that now he would sign it?" I asked.

"Yes, he did," said Trooper Bradley. "But he was being handcuffed during that part of the conversation."

Another lesson learned immediately on that aspect of the job. I had to write a memorandum to my sergeant about the incident, and for the next twenty-five years no one received more than one warning for failing to sign a citation. Over the years, I had to take several non-signers to jail, but one warning usually worked to resolve the issue.

Years later, I pulled over two young women on US 95 north of Winnemucca and wrote a citation to the driver. After asking the driver to sign the citation, she refused. As soon as I gave her the one and only warning of what would happen if she continued down this path, her friend in the passenger seat said, "Believe me, you want to sign the citation! I tried that once in Nevada, and I was in jail so fast it seemed like a blur!"

Many states do not require a signature on citations anymore, Nevada included, but for those states that still do, just sign the darn thing, or it will cause you hours of unnecessary self-imposed grief.

Opal Thieves

It was the summer of 1981, and I was patrolling Nevada State Route 140 about thirty miles east of Denio when my dispatch center requested that I respond to the Denio Junction Motel and Restaurant concerning the theft of ten thousand dollars' worth of opals from a local mine. The Humboldt County Sheriff's Office dispatcher advised that two white males suspected of stealing the opals were drinking at the bar and that the closest deputy responding to investigate the crime was still an hour away. I was asked to try and locate the two suspected thieves and detain them until the deputy arrived. This portion of northwestern Nevada is so remote that me getting there before these two guys could drive off was key to resolving this alleged theft.

Thirty miles west of Denio is an isolated area called Virgin Valley which is home to several mines that produce some of the finest opals on earth. The most famous of the Virgin Valley opal mines are the two oldest—the "Royal Peacock" and the "Rainbow Ridge." The world's most famous black fire opal, the "Roebling Opal" was mined there in 1918. Weighing in at 2,610 carats (about 1 ½ pounds) and valued at $250,000 in 1920, this beautiful opal has a permanent home in the Smithsonian Institution's famed Gem Hall in Washington D.C.

I was thirty-two miles east of Denio when I received the call to assist and arrived at the Junction just before noon. I walked into the bar expecting to see two desperados sitting on stools, but except for the bartender the place was empty.

"Are the two guys that you were trying to keep at the bar still around?" I asked.

"They just walked out the back door a couple of minutes ago," she said. "I tried to keep them here, but they were intent on leaving. I told them they needed to stay because the police officers wanted to talk to them, but that made them move even faster!"

I walked out the door and saw two guys getting into a dirty, green 1982 Chevy Blazer parked at the gas pumps near the front entrance. I had little information to go on other than what the owner of the mine had reported earlier that day—that two white males driving a green Chevy Blazer had stolen ten thousand dollars' worth of opals from his mine shop the afternoon before.

As I walked toward the men, I hollered, "Hey, guys, hold up a minute. I need to talk to you."

Both men stepped from their vehicle and waited as I approached. The driver appeared to be in his late-thirties, and the passenger a younger man in his mid-twenties. Rural Nevada troopers often work alone since backup is nonexistent or in short supply, so learning to be vigilant, thorough, and patient is key to survival.

With both suspects out of their vehicle where weapons could easily be retrieved, the first order of business was to separate them. I moved each a short distance away from the other and patted them down for weapons. Once certain that neither was armed, I informed them both that I was holding them for questioning in the alleged burglary of the Rainbow Ridge Opal Mine. I advised each of their Miranda Rights and ran wants and criminal histories on them as we waited for the deputy to arrive. The older suspect had an extensive criminal history with multiple felony convictions and had served time in prison. The younger man had a couple of misdemeanors, but nothing too serious on his record.

Deputy Stan Rorex, a good friend of mine, finally arrived and filled me in on what he knew up to that point. These two men had visited the Rainbow Ridge Opal Mine the afternoon before. Claiming to be rockhounds and showing a great interest in opals, they asked the owner, Keith Hodson, to show them around. Mr. Hodson gave them a tour of his property and took them into his office where he showed them glass vials containing beautiful fire opals suspended in oil, which is necessary to keep them from drying out. Mr. Hodson believed that while one kept him busy and distracted, the other was pocketing his opals. Right after the men left, Mr. Hodson noticed some of the vials missing. Earlier in their conversation, the two men had told Mr. Hodson that they were camping at the Virgin Valley Campground, so the next day an extremely irritated Mr. Hodson drove to a place where he had a view of the campground and the green Chevy Blazer. After the two men drove off, Mr. Hodson went to their campsite where he spotted broken glass vials and oil in the fire pit. That was when he called the sheriff's office to report the theft.

We certainly did not convey any of this information to the two men who admitted to visiting the mine but denied taking any opals. They consented to us searching their vehicle, so we went through every part of it and everything in it and found no opals. We were not surprised since the bartender had told them before I arrived that the police were coming to talk to them, giving them a few minutes to ditch the opals.

The only things of interest we found in the vehicle were a couple of large knives and a small television. I had been a trooper about seven months, and this was the only time in my career where being an inexperienced rookie actually paid off. I knew that any items with a serial number that are stolen or involved in a crime anywhere in America can be entered into the National Crime Information Center (NCIC) computer. Both knives and the television had serial numbers on them, so I ran them through NCIC, and dispatch advised that one of the knives had been reported stolen by a police department in New Jersey. I advised each of the men that the knife was reported stolen back east, cuffed them, and placed them under arrest in my car. Both men seemed incredibly surprised, one stating over and over that there was no way the knife could have been stolen. I transported them one hundred miles back to Winnemucca and booked them into different cells in the Humboldt County Jail for the night. Deputy Rorex stayed in the area for a while to meet with Mr. Hodson at the opal mine and continue the investigation.

Early the next morning, I met Deputy Rorex at the jail where he informed me that a Denio Junction employee had found a plastic bag containing beautiful fire opals in a trash can in the women's restroom. The owners of Denio Junction, Lee and Nancy Greenstreet, were keeping the opals safe until we could pick them up.

We decided to interview both suspects, starting with the older of the two since he was a career criminal and less likely to answer any questions. We made sure to walk the older crook directly past the younger crook's cell and make enough noise that the younger crook could not miss us moving his partner to the interview room. We informed the older, career crook of his rights. As expected, he didn't want to say anything or answer any questions and requested a lawyer, so there the three of us sat for over an hour, awkwardly staring at each other without saying a word.

Afterwards, we walked the older guy back to his cell in full view of his younger partner and then grabbed the younger man and walked him into the interview room. We immediately informed him of his Miranda Rights, and he stated that he wanted to talk and answer questions. He was being careful and was not giving up any information until we told him that his friend had sung like a bird. We had the opals from the restroom trash, the broken vials from their fire pit, and the other guy had given him up as the thief. That was when the younger crook told the story in its entirety.

After leaving the jail, I was informed that while NCIC confirmed that the knife had been stolen the day before, it turned out that the number I'd read off the knife was a model number, not a serial number, so the knife was not stolen. There were thousands of knives with that same model number. The police agency should not have listed the knife stolen using that number, and I was a rookie and didn't know the difference.

Both thieves were convicted in district court, and Mr. Hodson told me one day outside the courtroom that I could come up to his mine and dig for opals anytime I wanted. Sadly, I never did. Mr. Hodson has passed away, but being somewhat of a rockhound, I might get up there and dig for a beautiful fire opal one day.

Rolling Roadblock

It was a warm and beautiful northern Nevada evening on July 4th, 1981, and it was not unusual that I was the only state trooper working swing shift in Winnemucca. The fireworks were just getting ready to begin at the Winnemucca City Park. Sergeant Curti had told me earlier that if I wanted to meet my family there and watch the fireworks, it was fine as long as I stayed on the radio and was available for calls.

Wouldn't you know it, before the first fireworks were lit, my radio went off. "7376, Elko."

"7376, Winnemucca City Park."

"7419 (Trooper Don Smith) is in pursuit of a stolen vehicle, eastbound Interstate Eighty from Lovelock. The vehicle is a green Chevy station wagon, stolen out of Richmond, California yesterday and is occupied by a lone white male adult. Pursuit speeds are ranging ninety to one hundred miles per hour. Time is 2042 hours."

"10-4, Elko. 10-76 (on the way)."

With no fireworks in my immediate future, I jumped in my patrol car and headed out of town in a hurry. Lovelock is seventy miles west of Winnemucca, and at 100 miles per hour it wouldn't take long for the pursuit to get to my area.

I pulled into the median on I-80, about fifteen miles west of Winnemucca, and stopped where I could see a good twenty miles to the west. The pursuit was on its way. Way off in the distance, I could see it coming as I stayed in constant radio contact with Trooper Smith.

32

Unexpectedly, Humboldt County Sheriff's Deputy Richard Formby pulled up next to me and stopped. He was working that evening and was dispatched to assist. I was quite pleased to have an extra hand. That made three to one, odds we weren't used to having when you work alone in the middle of rural Nevada.

Deputy Formby and I formulated a plan. When the pursuit got about a mile or two west of us, we would both pull out onto the eastbound side of the interstate with our red and blue flashing emergency lights on. Deputy Formby would take the fast lane, and I would take the righthand slow lane. We would increase our speed while driving side by side, blocking both lanes, forcing the bad guy to slow down. Sort of a "Rolling Roadblock."

The driver of that green station wagon traveling at 100 miles per hour saw us in front and had nowhere to go! He could have certainly hit the brakes and slowed down or stopped, but he obviously didn't choose either of those two options. We were side by side, traveling about 35 mph, when the green wagon hit the rear end of Deputy Formby's patrol car. It was like that old game of clackers where you had two ceramic balls on a rope and when you drop one the other takes off. In less than the blink of an eye, Deputy Formby's patrol car shot down the road with its bumper, trunk, and backseat shoved right up behind the driver's seat. The green station wagon, with a scrunched-up front end was now directly beside me. Quite surprised, I considered my next move and decided to ram the right side of the station wagon with my patrol car, but before I could, Deputy Formby laid on the brakes of his patrol car. The station wagon struck the rear of the patrol car again, although with a lot less force. As a cloud of black smoke from hot brakes and smoking tires rose around both vehicles, Deputy Formby brought both cars to a stop.

Meanwhile, I was sliding to a stop directly beside the station wagon, relaying the situation to dispatch over the radio, getting my

12-gauge shotgun out of the rack, and trying to watch the bad guy. A very surprised Trooper Smith, directly behind the suspect, used every trick in the book to keep from hitting the whole sorry mess, laying down 100+ feet of locked-wheel skids. I guess the only one who wasn't surprised by the whole series of events was the bad guy.

The three of us were armed and out of our patrol cars immediately. The suspect had a rifle in his lap but never raised it. As soon as we got him out of the stolen car and handcuffed, Deputy Formby hit the ground. He'd taken one hell of a hit and left the scene by ambulance. Trooper Smith took the apparently uninjured suspect to jail, and while I sat there waiting for a tow truck to arrive, I had plenty of time to think about the terribly unsuccessful "Rolling Roadblock."

Stupid idea? You bet it was! There is no worse place to be in a pursuit than in front of a bad guy trying to get away in a car. I was at his mercy with absolutely no control over what he chose to do. It was a horrible position to be in.

Deputy Formby was off work for a couple of months with a multitude of soft-tissue injuries. Trooper Smith was the hero for arresting a bad guy and recovering a stolen vehicle. Trooper Raabe got to explain to his sergeant and lieutenant, who were not the least bit sympathetic, how this whole mess came about.

Never, never, never did I purposefully place my precious fanny in front of any bad guy again. And I made darn sure to tell the troopers who I supervised the rest of my career to never put themselves in that type of position or they would be explaining themselves at my desk.

Here's the Butter

State troopers spend a great amount of their time investigating and cleaning up traffic accidents and collisions. Those involving serious injury or death can take days or weeks to process and reach a conclusion. Collisions involving minor injuries or property damage are completed much sooner.

The exception to the quick rule for minor injury/property damage accidents are commercial vehicles where the load has spilled. If troopers are called to respond to a commercial vehicle accident where the trailer has rolled over, split open, dropped its contents, the load has shifted, or any number of related outcomes, they had better take a sandwich because they are going to be there a long time.

Most every driver has either been delayed or forced to detour around a commercial vehicle accident. Usually, if the trailer is intact, the load must be offloaded, sometimes by hand, to another trailer. If the contents have spilled, they must be cleaned up, sometimes by hand. If the load is destroyed, it will often be written off by an insurance company. If the damaged load contains anything consumed by humans, from apples to zucchini (and everything in between), it is condemned by the state or local health department. Now, in both circumstances, the contents are cleaned up and hauled off to the local dump and disposed of, even if some of the items have come through in perfect condition, but that hasn't always been the case. When I was a new trooper, whenever the health department condemned a trailer full of food items, much of it that was still good made its way to local people's tables (sometimes my own) instead of the dump. It wasn't until years later that the highway patrol said no more to that.

I have handled hundreds of truck wrecks carrying everything from concentrated grape juice (which left a lovely purple lake in the median) to swinging beef, hydrogen peroxide, cattle, tennis shoes, lye, household items, furniture, sheep, and the list goes on. The one that turned out to be extra fun was the load of butter.

It was a hot July morning in 1982 when I was dispatched to a commercial vehicle accident on I-80 at the 178-mile marker eastbound, which was within the Winnemucca city limits. I was the only trooper working in Winnemucca the entire day because our sergeant, Mike Curti, had scheduled everyone else off in the afternoon to attend the Winnemucca District summer picnic, hosted by the sarge and his wife Mary Lou, so clearly the wreck was mine to handle.

I arrived at one heck of a mess. There were scores of broken open cubes of butter melting all over the highway. Many were crushed and had been run over by the accident vehicle itself and by others that plowed through them before I arrived. I am not talking about ¼-pound cubes of butter, four of which make up a pound package that you buy at your local grocery store. These cubes were about two-foot square cubes of institutional butter packed in giant cardboard boxes weighing forty pounds apiece. The freeway was as slippery as a snowstorm in December with cars spun out everywhere.

I closed all eastbound traffic and contacted the highway department to bring a front-end loader and sand trucks. The only other times that I can remember needing sand trucks in the summer was when the highways were slick with squished Mormon cricket guts as billions of them migrated across the northern Nevada desert.

Once traffic was stopped and under control, it was time to figure out what happened. There was no damage to the tractor or the outside of the trailer. As the commercial vehicle was driving down I-80, the rotten floor of the trailer had simply given way due to the weight of the cubes of butter. The large butter boxes caused minor damage to many of the vehicles that ran them over which added to my workload as each strike was a separate accident report. Even with the help of the highway department, cleaning up the mess took the rest of my shift.

Five o'clock that evening, I loaded my young family into the car and headed to Sergeant Curti's house for our summer picnic. Each of us had chipped in for the steaks, and the sarge asked that each trooper's family bring a side dish. What made this wreck so memorable is that earlier that week Sergeant Curti had asked me to bring the rolls and butter.

I walked into Sergeant Curti's kitchen, flopped a big bag of fresh rolls on his kitchen counter, and said, "Here's the rolls, Sarge."

Then I went out to my car and returned with a forty-pound, two-foot cube box and said, "And here's the butter!"

I explained my day to my coworkers, and we all had a big laugh. At the end of the night, we divided the butter, and everyone went home with several pounds.

Missing Armrest

O h, what a busy day it had been. I started at 4:00 a.m., located a stolen car, booked the two kids in possession of it into the juvenile center in Winnemucca, returned to the highway, had completed two traffic stops and was on my third twenty-five miles west of Winnemucca on I-80 when I noticed a problem.

The problem was my armrest was missing. My elbow, searching for its normal place of rest, didn't stop where it should have and continued in a downward direction. I know what you're thinking. How big of a problem is a missing armrest? And you would be right if it was the armrest in my patrol car, but it wasn't. The armrest for my right elbow, often used while writing traffic citations to violators, was the large wooden butt (also called the pistol grip) of my .357 Smith & Wesson, Model 19 revolver. The bigger problem now was there was an idiot highway patrol trooper loose on the interstate without a gun—nothing but an empty holster, red face, rapidly beating heart, and a dry mouth.

So where was my armrest? Still in the lockbox at the Leighton Hall Juvenile Detention Center right where I left it. Anytime an officer goes into any type of jail facility, they must remove and lock up their firearm. Most jails place these handy little steel gun boxes right at the outside entrance door, making it hard for officers to leave without them. But not so at Leighton Hall, where it was situated in a most inconvenient place.

My lack of a gun kept getting more problematic. Now, this idiot trooper without a sidearm was thirty miles from town and the only one working for at least a hundred miles in any direction. Furthermore, he was not about to advise dispatch of his dilemma over the radio. It's one thing to be stupid, and quite another to tell the whole world about it.

The only solution was to finish issuing the citation, drive to town as fast as I possibly could, and retrieve it. While heading east toward Winnemucca, I remember hoping beyond hope that dispatch wouldn't send me to a call, but if it had to happen, please let it be east or north of Winnemucca, requiring me to travel through town.

I was ten miles west of Winnemucca when the highway patrol radio crackled, and dispatch said, "6144, Elko."

Always answering with one's present location, I picked up the radio and answered, "Elko, 6144. I-80, mile marker 166."

"6144, we have a report of a man down on the side of Interstate 80, westbound, mile marker 173."

"10-4. I am seven miles west and 10-76."

Darn. I was so close. All I needed was another fifteen minutes. A man down at 10:30 in the morning. What exactly did that mean? Was he drunk? Injured? Hit by a car? Sleeping? Whatever it was, I was handling it without a gun in my holster. I had a 12-gauge shotgun and an AR-15 in my car, but neither were handy to haul around unless they were really needed.

I arrived at the call and observed a ratty old sleeping bag in the dirt about fifteen feet off the edge of the highway. Sticking out of the top of the bag was a great big bush of mussed-up hair obviously belonging to the person inside. I grabbed my nightstick, which is a great tool but nothing you want to bring to a gunfight, approached the sleeping bag, and gave it a gentle poke.

"Hey. highway patrol! Are you alright?"

An older gentlemen stuck his head out of the bag and asked, "What's up?"

"I am Trooper Raabe," I said. "I was sent out her to check on you and see if you are okay."

"Yes, sir," he said. "I am just fine."

That's all I needed to hear. I finished the assignment in record time, continued to Winnemucca, and completed my immediate task.

Cops always tell stories of forgetting their guns in jail lockup. I know it has happened to others, and it is a horrible feeling, especially after you have completed a few traffic stops without it. For me, it was the one and only time in my career where I failed to retrieve my sidearm after booking a prisoner. Never again did I leave my armrest anywhere other than in its holster where it belonged.

Open Mouth, Insert Foot

It seemed like every fire season in northern Nevada came with the prediction of being the worst. If winter and spring were unusually wet, the resulting excess in vegetation meant more fuel and a bad year. If the winter and spring were unusually dry, the existing vegetation would be dry and catch fire easier which meant it was going to be a bad year. Not being a fireman, I can't tell you why the summer of 1982 was such a bad fire year, but 757,000 acres burned, and large portions of Humboldt County were on fire.

One afternoon in mid-July, I was patrolling west of Winnemucca on I-80 when I noticed smoke and flames at the Thacker Ranch about a mile north of the Cosgrave Rest Area. I advised my dispatch center in Elko of the situation and asked that they contact the nearest fire department and have them respond. I proceeded down the dirt road to the ranch house where no one appeared to be home. The homestead was located close to the railroad tracks, and two large outbuildings were totally engulfed in flames. The first transcontinental railroad (also called the Pacific Railroad) was completed across Nevada in 1869. Many of the ranch buildings in the area were constructed of old, creosote-soaked railroad ties, and they burned like torches.

About forty-five minutes later, I looked up and saw a fire engine coming down the dirt road with its lights on and sirens blaring. It had Imlay Volunteer Fire Department on the door and appeared to be a very old model, more like an antique. I didn't even know that the tiny, non-incorporated town of Imlay had a fire department. Considering that Imlay was twenty miles away, their fire department was completely staffed by volunteers, and the firetruck likely didn't exceed fifty miles per hour their response time was pretty good.

The engine stopped a safe distance from the burning buildings, and the two firemen got out of the engine—an obese middle-aged woman and a skinny kid who appeared to still be in his teens. Now, looks can be deceiving, and I had no reason to think that these two firefighters could not handle the situation; it just wasn't what I expected to see.

Both immediately went to work dragging hoses, flipping switches, and turning knobs. Meanwhile, the fire had spread to the adjacent sagebrush and greasewood. I waited and waited and waited for the water to flow, but it just wasn't happening.

After twenty minutes of watching the firefighters do their best with no results, I noticed a nice-looking Bureau of Land Management helicopter circling the area looking for a place to land. The helicopter sat down, and two men climbed out and walked over to where I was standing. One of them introduced himself as the BLM fire supervisor for the entire northern part of the state. As he looked around, I asked him, "How long before one of your fire crews shows up?"

"Well," he said, "this fire is on private property, so I won't be sending a crew."

"Sir," I said, "I don't know if you have noticed or not, but my fire department has been here for over half an hour, and they have not managed to get one drop of water out of the end of that hose. As soon as this fire crosses that fenceline fifty feet away, it is going to be on federal land and belong to you."

"Okay," he said, "I will get a crew on the way."

The helicopter took off, and I was sent on a call miles away, so I never actually got to see who put the fire out. The next day, I was on patrol in the same area and asked the new Pershing County deputy, who had recently moved to Imlay, to meet for coffee.

During our break, the deputy named John asked, "Are you the trooper that responded to the fire at the Thacker Ranch yesterday?"

"Yes, and it was something to see," I said. "The Imlay Volunteer Fire Department rolled up, and a fat lady and a kid got out. They worked like hell to get that old fire truck to squirt water, but I doubt they got it to work. After an hour or so I had to leave, so I'm not sure if they put the fire out or if the BLM saved the day."

Deputy John looked at me and said, "BLM put the fire out, and that fat lady is my wife!"

"Well, there you have it," I said. "Open mouth, insert foot." My new acquaintance was smiling from ear to ear, and I asked, "You're just screwing with me, right?"

"No, I'm afraid I'm not," he said. "That was my wife."

All I could think of to say was, "Well, she wasn't that fat!" and both of us exploded in laughter.

Both John and his wife were wonderful people, our families and children became very good friends, and we spent a lot of time together. John died quite young from a heart attack, leaving a great woman and three children. Thankfully, they had a lot of family and support in that part of Nevada. To this day, anytime I think of that coffee break, I smile. My friend John was quick to smile and had a great laugh and a wonderful sense of humor, which helped to alleviate one of the most embarrassing moments of my life.

Speeding to Catch Speeders

When I started as a highway patrol trooper in 1980, radar was a very important tool for speed enforcement on Nevada's highways. Like any new traffic trooper, I couldn't wait to get my hands on a radar, but department policy did not allow new troopers to have one until they completed one year on the road enforcing the multitude of other traffic laws in existence and had passed radar school. In mid-1982, after a year and a half working the highway, I was finally able to attend radar school.

Radar stands for "Radio Detection and Ranging." Many inventors like Christian Hulsmeyer and Guglielmo Marconi had a hand in discovering and improving early radar, but in 1935 it was British physicist, Sir Robert Watson-Watt, who first produced a practical radar system that just five years later, quite early in World War II, was able to detect enemy aircraft approaching England over a distance of eighty miles. Rest assured that by the time I was allowed to get my mitts on a radar, they were extremely accurate. But even then, I had my doubts.

I learned more about radar over that week of training than I thought possible. After understanding how and why radar works, my faith in it grew exponentially. The radar is reliable and dead-on accurate, so much so that unlike a polygraph machine, radar readings are allowed in court. If there is a problem with a radar reading, it is very easy to spot if the operator is trained to do so. That is why our department requires every operator to attend and pass radar school, be adept at estimating vehicle speeds and distances, pass initial certification, and be recertified every two years.

After passing radar school, students spend several weeks on the highway obtaining hundreds of required target vehicle clocks. The student selects a target vehicle, estimates the vehicle's distance away in feet, starts a stopwatch, estimates the vehicle's speed, obtains its actual speed using radar, stops the watch when the vehicle passes the patrol car, computes the actual distance the target vehicle traveled using a mathematical formula, then records the vehicle description and all the data onto a department radar clocking form. Students are required to perform these clocks from both parked and moving patrol cars. Students are allowed to stop and warn speeding drivers while obtaining their radar clocks but are not allowed to issue speeding citations until certified to do so. Obtaining radar clocks is both monotonous and time-consuming, but necessary to teach new troopers to use radar.

After all the radar clock forms are turned into the radar instructor, it is time for certification. The radar instructor jumps in the passenger seat of your patrol car, covers up the radar so you can't see it, and tests your ability to accurately judge target speed and distance.

Here's an example of how this process goes.

The instructor will pick a target vehicle and say, "That red truck coming at you. What is its speed and distance now?"

The instructor starts the stopwatch, and the student states the vehicle's estimated speed and distance at, for example, "900 feet at 74 miles per hour."

The instructor records the actual speed and computes the actual distance of each target and documents all the estimates and actual numbers onto a certification form. This nerve-wracking action goes on for hours. At the end of the day, if the student does not estimate speeds and distances within a certain passing percentage of accuracy, they are not certified to operate radar and they start the target vehicle clocking process all over again, which can be very disheartening.

I want you to imagine sitting in a patrol car checking the speed of hundreds of vehicles every day of your working life. Believe me when I tell you that experienced state troopers know how fast you are driving within a mile or two just by looking at you without using a radar. The radar just confirms the estimate and gives the trooper the exact speed, rather than a very close guess.

After school, certification, and working with that miraculous little machine every day for twenty-plus years, I would bet my life on it. Every experienced Nevada trooper had a radar-equipped patrol car, but I had never seen one in anything other than a patrol car until one morning when I was working on I-80.

I was about four miles east of Winnemucca when I saw a passenger vehicle speeding eastbound. I estimated the vehicle speed at 81 miles per hour, and the radar confirmed the speed at 82 mph in a 55-mph speed zone. I stopped the vehicle, and while conversing with the middle-aged male driver, I observed an older model handheld radar called a "Speed Gun 8" sitting beside him on the front seat. I was curious as to why this guy would have a radar in his car, so I asked him. The driver told me he was the Union Pacific Railroad trainmaster, and he was trying to get ahead of an eastbound train to check its speed. The trainmaster believed that the engineer was exceeding the railroad speed limit, and that it was his job to catch him.

"Sir, let me get this straight," I said. "You're telling me, a guy whose job it is to catch you speeding, that you are traveling on this highway at twenty-seven miles per hour over the posted speed limit so you can catch someone else speeding?"

Repeating that comment back to him made him realize just how stupid it sounded and conveyed to him in so many words that there was no way he was getting out of this situation without a citation, which he received.

I would have loved to share this story with my best friend Dennis Mastin, who was a Union Pacific Railroad conductor in Winnemucca, but I was never the type to write and tell.

Here, Take the Keys

I was sitting stationary on the side of I-80 at the top of Golconda Summit when I noticed a car drive past me with expired Nevada license plates, so I entered the highway and caught up to him in a hurry. When I turned on the overhead lights, the driver's instantaneous reaction was a bit of a surprise. He abruptly pulled to the right road edge, and I barely managed to get stopped behind him without denting his rear bumper. The surprises didn't stop there.

The driver stepped out of his vehicle as quickly as I did, and he pitched his car keys at me and yelled, "Here, take the keys!"

Being a Babe Ruth baseball all-star in my teens, I easily caught the hurled keys and tossed them back, saying, "I don't want your keys."

He immediately threw them back at me and said, "No, you take them. I don't want the damn things."

As I tossed them back again, I said, "I don't want the keys. What the hell is wrong with you?"

One more time, he tossed them at me and said, "I was just stopped a half hour ago by the Winnemucca Police Department and received a warning for having expired registration. The officer told me I was lucky that he stopped me because if I had been stopped by the highway patrol, they would impound my car. They must have called you and told you I was headed this way, so you can take the car and keep it."

State troopers look at every license plate that goes by, and the wrong-colored sticker in the upper-right corner is a dead giveaway. Thanks a lot, Winnemucca P.D. No one told me this guy was coming, but they sure had gotten him riled up for the next trooper that stopped him—me.

"Nobody called me," I said. "And while your registration appears to have expired last year, I have no intention of impounding your car, so just settle down."

This seemed to calm the guy down a little. After the game of catch ended, the traffic stop took on the semblance of normality.

After checking that the local man had no warrants for his arrest and that he had a valid Nevada driver's license, I turned him loose with a citation for expired registration.

Quite often, rural Nevada troopers who always work alone have coffee or lunch with local deputies and city officers. The next time I met with them, I asked them to please not rile up my violators. They laughed, but since most cops are pranksters, I think my plea fell on deaf ears.

Our Professions Have Similarities

The state of Nevada, my home for most of my life, has many things that set it apart from most other states. First is size. Nevada is the seventh-largest state and ninth-lowest in population density. Second is the city of Las Vegas that has few, if any, comparisons. Third are our Nevada mountain ranges which greatly outnumber those in all other states except for Alaska. Lastly, I will mention the one thing Nevada has that no other state allows—legalized prostitution.

One may think it weird to discuss such a topic, but for those of us who were raised in Nevada, it is not abnormal or strange. It is a legitimate business that is taxed, regulated, and controlled by both state and local governments. While prostitution is legal, there are still many laws on the Nevada books governing what has been called "the world's oldest profession." It is allowed on a county-by-county basis and only in counties that do not exceed 400,000 in population, so it is not legal in Reno or Las Vegas. It is only legal in state-licensed brothels and not allowed on the street, on Craigslist, in private residences, in hotel rooms, or for trade. Currently, prostitution is legal in ten of Nevada's seventeen counties, and the number of brothels has become fewer in number than years past.

Since it is a legitimate business in our state, no one should be surprised to know that our two professions, prostitution and law enforcement, occasionally crossed paths. The Moonlight Bunny Ranch was a sponsor for our Nevada Highway Patrol Association Golf Tournament in Carson City for several years, even though our chief wasn't particularly happy about it. Employees from the brothel supplied silent auction items and gave gifts (all in good taste) to winners of the tournament. We have also had prostitutes involved in traffic accidents, which is how we discovered that our two professions had quite a bit in common.

In the winter of 1984, Sergeant Mike Curti handled a motor vehicle accident in a snowstorm near Winnemucca that resulted in serious injuries to the female driver who was an employee of the Calico Club in the town of Battle Mountain. The lady was taken to Reno by ambulance, and Sergeant Curti never had the chance to meet up with her, so a month later he sent a memo and a copy of a citation to the highway patrol office in Battle Mountain asking that Corporal Bill Souza see to it that it was delivered and signed.

The memos went as follows:

May 2, 1984
To: Corporal Bill Souza
From: Sergeant Mike Curti
Subject: Enclosed Citation
Could you please have this citation delivered and signed. (Lady's name) works at the Calico Club. Please send your most reliable state trooper. She works there as a hostess? a bartender? or something!
Thanks for taking care of this for me.
P.S. The trooper that takes this citation will be timed.

May 10, 1984
To: Sergeant Mike Curti
From: Corporal Bill Souza
Subject: Citation served
Per your request to serve citation #A332456 on (lady's name).

Trooper Harmon was assigned the task because of his ability to accomplish assignments under unusual circumstances. After a brief visit, Trooper Harmon returned to the office with a somewhat perplexed yet satisfied look on his face.

Since I was preparing his next evaluation, I inquired as to what transpired during his brief and timed visit to the Calico Club. Apparently, he and some of the employees started discussing their respective job descriptions and work-performance standards. He, in turn, discussed them with me.

After more consideration, I am surprised at the similarities involved between the world's oldest profession and law enforcement and have decided there are standards for both industries. I have made a short list for your convenience.

Professionals in both fields realize that if you can successfully deal with a truck driver, you can probably deal with anybody.

Call to duty often involves working late night hours.

Productivity generates revenue.

Speed is a factor in both professions. They speed people up for the sake of time, and we use our time to slow people down.

Negotiation is key. Their clients are always trying to talk their way into something, where our clients are always trying to talk their way out.

Training is important, but experience is what really counts.

Neither profession is overpaid.

Both professions require undercover work.

Both professions handle accidents.

Both occupations have been described as long tedious hours of boredom interspersed with moments of pure excitement.

From time to time, members of both professions get screwed.

Yes, we worked hard, but we never missed a chance at a little fun. As for legalized prostitution in our state, someone is always parading around trying to end it. Quite often, people and groups from other states. For those of us who were raised here, it is like any other legal business, and a fact of Nevada life.

What Are You Doing?

Every Saturday night in the summer, stock car races were held at the Winnemucca fairgrounds. Located just off the south side of I-80 and situated lower than the highway, cars that stopped and parked on the eastbound side of the interstate had the best seats in the house. Keeping folks from congregating there required several visits to the area every race night.

The other problem was that after watching race cars zooming around all night, there were always a couple of frustrated spectators who left the fairgrounds racing their vehicles down the highway. Expecting to see several wannabe Mario Andretti's after the race, I parked my patrol car about a block from the entrance to the highway and waited.

Within minutes, a purple, two-door Dodge Charger made a tire-squealing left turn onto the highway, fishtailing as it proceeded in the opposite direction. Traffic was heavy, so by the time I got safely through the intersection, the Charger was two little taillights far off in the distance. The Charger was approaching the I-80 eastbound on-ramp, so at least it was headed for my turf. The first little town it would come to was Golconda, fifteen miles east, meaning I would have plenty of time to catch it.

I was driving a 1982 Plymouth Fury ll, which was most likely to win the award for worst patrol car ever made. The moron in highway patrol headquarters that ordered those wrecks should have been tarred and feathered. It had a terrible habit of vapor locking every time it overheated, which was often. Vapor lock was when the liquid fuel would turn to gas while in the fuel delivery system, resulting in a stalled engine. It was also so underpowered and slow that it had difficulty getting out of its own way.

After what seemed like an eternity, I finally hit the interstate in pursuit of the Charger. I got my rotten patrol car up to about 110 miles per hour, which was no easy feat, and I could still see the even smaller taillights a mile or so ahead. I had no radar clock on the vehicle, so I had no idea how fast it was going.

There are several accepted ways to check the speed of vehicles, such as pacing, radar, the older VASCAR systems, and Sky Timers used in enforcement from an aircraft. VASCAR and Sky Timers simply and accurately compute speed by dividing a known distance traveled by the time it takes to do so. Pacing is following a violator's vehicle and matching your speed with its speed for a reasonable distance. When pacing another vehicle, it must be done in stealth mode. There is no way to pace a suspected speeder if the patrol car emergency and strobe lights are lit up like a Christmas tree.

So, there I was, streaking across the desert at 110 mph in a 55-mph zone, attempting to pace the purple Charger, when all of a sudden a pickup truck changes lanes to pass another vehicle with absolutely no signal. Oh crap! There he was, directly in front of me in the left lane, the vehicle he was passing in the right lane, and me with no place to go.

I slammed on the brakes and laid down several hundred feet of tire-smoking, highway-smearing, locked-wheel skids. Of course, being a certified accident reconstruction expert, I know when a vehicle's brakes are locked up there is no steering, but it didn't matter because there was nowhere to steer anyway.

How I didn't slam into the back of that pickup, I'll never know. Young fast reflexes, perfect timing, a disgustingly slow patrol car, and luck saved the day. Now all my attention was transferred from "Mario Andretti" to "Mr. Can't Use a Blinker."

I regained my composure, turned all my fancy emergency lights on, and pulled the pickup over. I approached the older male driver and asked, "What on earth are you doing changing lanes without signaling?"

The man's sarcastic response was, "What on earth are you doing driving so fast out here without any emergency lights on?"

Legally, while on patrol, we had the right to disregard any and all traffic laws in the pursuit of violators, or when responding to emergencies. There are a few situations when it is not advisable for law enforcement to use lights and sirens, like when responding to a robbery in progress, a home invasion, a violent domestic dispute, or when pacing a speeder across the wide-open desert on a hot summer night, but that does not relieve the officer of responsibility should they hit or injure someone while doing so. Had I slammed into the back of that truck, it would have been as much my fault as his. It is a fine line for an officer to walk.

So, having been so eloquently and shrewdly one-upped, I made a deal with the driver. If he promised to use his blinker, I would promise to use more care while chasing violators. I said a quick goodnight, tucked my tail between my legs, returned to my rotten patrol car, grateful that it didn't go any faster. The entire affair ended with a big fat zero in the ticket department, but I was reminded of just how dangerous my job could be to both me and the motoring public.

Harvey's in the Camper

A warm, beautiful, quiet, dark, Sunday night in the Nevada desert, and I knew it wouldn't last. About the time you think how lucky you are that nothing is going on, dispatch calls, and off you go, so we tried not to talk about it.

Sundays and Tuesdays on I-80 in northern Nevada were always busy with commercial trucks. On Sundays, the trucks were headed west to pick up loads in California on Monday. The vast majority traveled through our area again on Tuesday, headed back east.

I was working near the little town of Golconda. My friend and coworker, Trooper Larry Reynolds, was working about twenty miles east of me, near the town of Battle Mountain. I heard his ID number as he called dispatch, and I could tell from his voice that something was going on.

"Elko, 6087, I am out with an older male, westbound, four miles east of Pumpernickel, who was run over by a westbound commercial vehicle. Requesting a 10-52 (ambulance) respond to my location."

I immediately headed east to assist Trooper Reynolds. Knowing he was quite busy, I didn't try to contact him by radio. Within a couple of minutes, Trooper Reynolds called dispatch to advise that the man had expired, to cancel the ambulance, and to contact the coroner and our sergeant, Mike Curti.

I asked Trooper Reynolds if he needed any help, and he said, "The guy just died, so there's nothing you can do here. I was driving westbound, following a half mile behind a commercial vehicle when I saw the taillights of the trailer bounce up and down like it had run over something. The commercial vehicle continued west, and as I came to the area, I noticed what looked like a bundle of rags in the travel lane. Then I realized that the bundle of rags was a person."

Since Trooper Reynolds had to render aid to the victim, he could not pursue the commercial vehicle that had failed to stop. He asked me to look for a westbound tractor/van trailer combination with possible front-end damage to the tractor. Keep in mind this was the busiest night of the week for westbound truck traffic. Short of setting up a roadblock to stop and visually inspect every westbound truck in the area, the chances of finding the vehicle that had run over this man were slim to none. The most we could hope for would be the driver reporting it or finding a commercial vehicle pulled over on the side of the highway with a driver looking for damage.

Sergeant Curti came on duty and met with Trooper Reynolds at the scene. There was nothing to go on concerning the truck, which by now was long gone, but they did find a driver's license on the body identifying the dead man as Harvey Knight of Winnemucca.

After the body was removed, Trooper Reynolds and Sergeant Curti cleared from the scene en route to Winnemucca for follow up. This particular follow up would include notifying Mr. Knight's family of his death and trying to find out why Mr. Knight was all alone in the middle of the desert and how he happened to be run over by a commercial vehicle.

I listened as my coworkers checked out on the radio at Mr. Knight's residence. A while later, they called and asked me to meet them for coffee. That is where I learned, as Paul Harvey Sr. used to say, "the rest of the story."

Sergeant Curti and Trooper Reynolds knocked on the front door of the Harvey residence. An older woman answered the door, and Sergeant Curti asked if she was Mrs. Harvey Knight. She said that she was.

Sergeant Curti said, "I am sorry to give you bad news, Mrs. Knight, but your husband Harvey was killed in a traffic accident tonight."

Mrs. Knight said, "No, that can't be. Harvey's in the camper!"

Sergeant Curti told Mrs. Knight, "The body of a man matching Mr. Knight's description and with identification showing him to be Mr. Harvey Knight was found dead on Interstate eighty."

Again, Mrs. Knight said, "It can't be Harvey. We just returned from Battle Mountain. Harvey's drunk, so he rode home in the back of the camper."

Mrs. Knight led Sergeant Curti and Trooper Reynolds to a cabover camper mounted on the back of her pickup truck and opened the door. You guessed it—the camper was empty.

Mrs. Knight said, "Harvey was passed out in the camper when we left Battle Mountain. I wonder where he went."

When asked if Harvey was riding alone in the camper, a surprised and distraught Mrs. Knight assured them that he was.

In Nevada, blood tests are required on all who pass away from non-natural causes. Tests revealed that Mr. Harvey Knight was extremely intoxicated when he died. Since there was no reason to believe, or evidence to indicate, that a third party tossed Harvey out the camper door, it was chalked up as an accidental death.

It is quite probable that an intoxicated Harvey Knight either walked right out, or fell out, the back door of the camper while traveling at sixty miles per hour. We would never know for sure, but two things were certain: It was Harvey's last night on planet earth and his last occasion to overindulge in alcohol.

Ralph Wolf and Sam Sheepdog

One of the joys of working as a state trooper was sharing the highways with commercial truck drivers. All of them had Citizens Band (CB) radios in their rigs and referred to us as Smokey Bear. There was no way for us to move anywhere on the highways of rural Nevada without countless truckers broadcasting to all others where we currently were or where we had recently been. This made it much more difficult to catch the ones who violated traffic laws like speeding, following too close, and unsafe lane changes.

Though our chosen careers and responsibilities made us adversaries at times, most commercial truck drivers were great men and women who watched out for us daily and jumped in to help when we needed a hand. Rural Nevada State troopers nearly always work alone far from any other officers, so the truckers we encountered were often all we had, and they knew it. Throughout my career, truckers helped me wrestle and arrest drunks, direct traffic at accident scenes, watch over injured accident victims, locate wrong way drivers, drunk drivers, stolen cars, and hit and run vehicles. More than a few followed directly behind my patrol car in raging snowstorms at night because their higher headlights provided a much better view for me in near-zero visibility. Driving big rigs across America is not an easy job, and though I ran into some bad ones and had to arrest a few, the vast majority had my respect and did an excellent job.

One of my favorite truck drivers of all time also happened to be my first father-in-law, Raymond Mack. His daughter, Deborah, and I were married very young. Though we didn't stay together, my friendship with Ray lasted a lifetime. He was one of my favorite people that I have shared this planet with. Over the years, we hunted, fished, bowled in leagues, and played more games of cribbage than I could count.

After years as a diesel mechanic and timber faller, Ray switched occupations and became a driver for Tri-State Motor Transport. Ray's truck-driving job brought him through Winnemucca often, and he would usually stay for a night or two before moving on. I had full-time custody of my three children, and Ray loved to spend time with his grandchildren as well.

On one of Ray's stopovers, he and I stayed up late playing cribbage. It was summer, and I was working the 4:00 a.m. until noon shift which I really liked because it allowed me to spend more time with my kids. The downside was that I never seemed to get to sleep early enough in the evening, making it a long and tiring month. About 11:00 p.m. I told Ray that I had to get a few hours of sleep before getting up at 3:00 a.m. for work.

"If you're getting up at three a.m. for work," Ray said, "I will too."

"Alright," I said. "I'll see you at three a.m., and we'll have coffee before we hit the road."

3:00 a.m. came early. Ray and I were having coffee and a great visit when I started to laugh. I had a thought about both of us going to work at the same time. Ray the truck driver trying to go fast and break the rules, and me the state trooper trying to catch him.

"Ray," I said, "this reminds me of the old cartoon about Ralph Wolf and Sam Sheepdog. They were the best of friends and greeted each other before work."

"Good morning, Sam," said Ralph.

"Good morning, Ralph," said Sam.

Both would punch in at the time clock, the work whistle would blow, and then the trouble began. Ralph tried to steal sheep, and Sam tried to stop him.

At 3:55 a.m. we both walked outside of the house and immediately went to work. All Ray had to do was climb into his truck and start the engine, and all I had to do was start my patrol car, turn on the radio, and tell dispatch I was on duty.

I immediately turned on my CB radio and called Ray. "Hey, trucker, this is Smokey Bear. Have you got your ears on?"

"10-4, Smokey. I got them on," Ray said.

"Well, driver," I said. "Since you drive a big old semi and I drive a fast little Ford Mustang, I am going to give you a fifteen-minute head start, then I'm coming after you!"

"Hey, Smokey," Ray said. "Do your best—better troopers have tried!"

I caught up to Ray on I-80 a few miles east of Winnemucca. We had a good time, laughing and joking with each other over our CB radios before he went his way and I went mine. I have known few better men than my one-time father-in-law and great friend, Raymond Mack, and though he has passed on, he will always hold a special place in my heart.

The Hell I Was

Thank you, Federal Government, in 1974, for imposing upon our western states the National Maximum Speed Law which restricted the maximum permissible vehicle speed limit to 55 miles per hour on all federally funded highways. The law was a response to the 1973 oil embargo, and its intent was to reduce fuel consumption. For our state of Nevada, which had never had a speed limit across our wide-open desert highways, the new law was hated by all, but none more so than by Nevada State troopers. We were the ones charged with the responsibility of slowing everyone down to a crawl.

The act prohibited the Department of Transportation from approving or funding any projects within states that did not comply with the new speed limit. The individual states were held hostage, and those with long highways and few residents were forced to comply.

Many people have heard of U.S. Highway 50, which crosses the central portion of Nevada. In 1986, *Life Magazine* named it "The Loneliest Road in America." While it is one of the least-traveled roads crossing America, it is not one of the loneliest roads crossing portions of Nevada. While many obscure state routes could vie for the title, Nevada State Route 140 would certainly be a contender.

SR 140 crosses 110.3 miles of northwestern Nevada, from its intersection with US 95 thirty-two miles north of Winnemucca to the state line east of Lakeview, Oregon. It is a very long, desolate highway with a few ranches and one tiny town near the middle called Denio. Crawling across this remote section of Nevada at fifty-five miles per hour is pure torture, so anytime I patrolled that stretch of highway, a driver really had to be speeding to warrant my attention, and occasionally one did.

One morning, I was on patrol westbound on a long, straight stretch of State Route 140 when I saw a lone vehicle several miles ahead approaching me eastbound. Out of habit, I hit the switch on my radar, releasing a radio wave at the speed of light. Traveling at 186,000 miles per second, the radio wave bounced off the target and returned instantaneously, showing a speed of 107 miles per hour. Anyone who is trained to operate radar knows that a reading taken on a target so far away couldn't possibly be used to issue a citation, so rather than locking in the reading, I continued to monitor the speed of the vehicle. As the vehicle came toward me, it showed a constant speed of 107 mph. From the constant reading, I knew the driver didn't have a radar detector and either hadn't seen me yet or didn't care.

As the vehicle shot past me, I turned in pursuit. The driver had seen me as he passed and pulled over to the right side of the two-lane highway and stopped. As I pulled in behind the car, I informed my dispatch center of my location and the vehicle description. I approached the car and met with an older gentleman who was driving and his wife who was his passenger. I obtained the man's driver's license and registration and told him that he was stopped for driving 107 mph in a 55-mph zone.

The man looked at me and said, "Young man, there's no way I was doing 107 miles per hour!"

"Sir," I replied, "I checked your car on radar as you approached me for several miles today, and it displayed a constant reading of 107 mph."

"I'm telling you, there's no way you could've checked me at 107. My speedometer read 115 mph all the way across the valley."

I smiled and said, "Well, sir, I beg to differ. My radar is a hundred times more accurate than your speedometer, and you were only going 107 mph."

"Well, hell," he said. "That's disappointing. Here I thought I was doing 115 mph. Are you sure?"

"Yes, sir. I'm positive."

"Well then, I guess I was going 107."

"Alright, I'll tell you what. You thought you were doing 115 miles per hour. I checked you at 107 miles per hour. The speed limit is 55. How about we split the difference on the citation at 82 miles per hour?"

"That sounds good to me."

I issued the man a citation and visited a while with one of the few drivers I would see that day on this lonely stretch of road. Both of us drove off smiling. Another happy customer.

KGA-637 New Jersey

Over the course of their career, American law enforcement officers fire their weapons at another person an average of 0.01 times, which is right next to zero. To put that in perspective, 1 out of 100 officers shoots at another person once during a thirty-year career. Believe me, if cops got shot at in real life like they do on television or in the movies, most of us would have changed professions in a hurry. I have shot many animals injured in accidents and fired thousands of rounds in training, but I never had to fire a weapon at a person—although I came close to doing so several times.

While firing a weapon is a rarity, drawing one and having it ready to fire is a common occurrence. Several times per month, officers pull out sidearms, shotguns, or semi-automatic rifles, depending on the situation. Anytime we were dealing with known felons or in dangerous situations, firearms would come out.

Quite often, we had no idea we were in a jam or dealing with dangerous individuals until our dispatch center told us so. The license plate of every vehicle we encountered was given to our dispatcher who would run it through NCIC (the National Crime Information Center) to see if said vehicle was stolen, involved in a felony crime, or occupied by a wanted criminal. If the vehicle license plate was listed in NCIC, dispatch would advise us by emitting a special tone over the radio. This was followed by special code words, the trooper's identification number, and their location. If we were safe in our vehicle, dispatch would readily give us the information. If we were already in contact with the potentially dangerous suspect, any pertinent information would not be relayed until the suspect was under control and the trooper was safe.

One morning, I was working on I-80 within the Winnemucca city limits and decided to make a traffic stop on a passenger vehicle I'd checked on radar at 68 miles per hour in a 55-mph speed zone. The vehicle was occupied by a lone male traveling eastbound.

I picked up the radio and said, "Elko, 6144, 10-6 (traffic stop)."

"6144."

"10-6, Interstate 80, mile marker 177 eastbound, on a red Dodge Charger with New Jersey registration KGA-637."

Dispatch replied, "10-4, 6144."

The vehicle pulled over immediately, and before my patrol car came to a complete stop, the special tone came over my radio, followed by, "Saint Thomas Elko, #6144 Frank, I-80, mile marker 177, eastbound."

I immediately drew my handgun and pointed it in the direction of the occupant. The occupants usually got a glimpse of a firearm pointed in their direction, and with few exceptions, most were quite amenable to following directions. Using my public address system, I advised the driver to follow my directions carefully and exactly as stated.

"Driver, place both hands in the air where I can see them. Do it now...."

"Driver, using your left hand, roll down the driver's side window. Do it now...."

"Driver, using your left hand, open the driver's door, and without looking in my direction, step from the vehicle. Do it now....

"Driver, while facing the front with both hands in the air, walk backwards toward the sound of my voice. Do it now...."

"Driver, stop and drop down to your knees. Do it now....

"Driver, lay on your stomach and stretch both arms out to your sides with your palms up, then cross your feet. Do it now....

Now that the lone male was prone on the ground and the situation was under control, it was time to contact dispatch and get the details. Up to this point, I had no idea what the felony situation was or what the person was wanted for. It could be anything from felony murder to writing bad checks or anything in between.

"Elko, 6144."

"6144."

"I have the single occupant of the vehicle prone on the ground and need to confirm the NCIC hit on New Jersey registration KGA-637."

"6144, I thought you said New Jersey KGA-367."

"Negative, Elko. New Jersey KGA-637!"

Several seconds went by before I heard, "6144, Elko. New Jersey KGA-637 shows no wants, negative NCIC, comes back registered on a Dodge Charger to so and so out of New Jersey."

This poor guy gets stopped for thirteen miles an hour over the speed limit and gets taken out of his car at gunpoint!

In the nicest voice I could invoke, I said, "Sir, go ahead and stand up."

To which, he replied, "I am not standing up until you put that gun away!"

"The gun is put away, and you can go ahead and stand up."

The guy stood up, and rather than try to give a lengthy explanation of what had just occurred, I simply stated that his car closely matched the description of a car being driven by a bad guy and offered a quick apology.

"Sir, the speed limit in our state is fifty-five miles per hour. We take speeding quite seriously, but I am just going to give you a warning today and expect you to slow down."

This guy was in as much of a hurry for this event to end as I was. Of the hundreds of felony traffic stops I made during my career, this was the only time that I made one on an undeserving motorist. There is a joke about the dyslexic highway patrolman who stopped a lady for drinking and gave her an I.U.D. I don't know if I called off the plate wrong or the dispatcher heard it wrong, but it really didn't matter. Either way, I bet the poor man from New Jersey kept his speed at 55 mph until he was safely into Utah!

The Bear in the Air

In the mid-1980s, the Nevada Highway Patrol purchased its first aircraft, a Cessna 182 RG (with retractable landing gear) that would be used for speed enforcement and other special operations as needed. I remember thinking that it was about time. I had watched the television show *ChiPs* for three years before becoming a state trooper. The show featured two actors portraying California Highway Patrol motor officers, Ponch and Jon, as they performed their daily tasks. In addition to riding cool police motorcycles, Ponch and Jon rode dirt bikes, jet skis, and ATVs, flew in hang gliders, helicopters, and airplanes, and even parachuted into the mountains to arrest bad guys. Knowing it was Hollywood, I never expected to ride a jet ski or parachute into the desert to catch a bad guy, but at least now, in addition to patrol cars and a few motorcycles, having one aircraft was a beginning for California's poor neighbor to the east.

Before long, troopers on patrol were watching highway department crews paint white outlines of an airplane and stripes (a quarter of a mile apart) on highways throughout the state. The few times I had flown in a small airplane I loved it, so when Aircraft Observer classes were scheduled for any troopers interested, I was first in line.

The Aircraft Observer class included aircraft operations and safety, seeing vs. observing, locating targets, search patterns, calling targets, detection and speed monitoring of vehicles, operating the speed-detection system Sky Timer, and lastly, dealing with the dreaded and common malady—air sickness.

For those troopers who passed the written exam, the day finally came to climb into the backseat of the NHP airplane and get certified on the Sky Timer. When my turn arrived, I proceeded to the Winnemucca Airport where I met long-time friend, trooper and pilot, Jim Allison. We flew directly to the nearest set of painted stripes on I-80 at the Rose Creek Interchange, not five miles from the airport. On the ground were two highway patrol cars that were to proceed through the speed-detection site at predetermined speeds while I checked their speeds from the air. The airplane would fly in tight circles 500 feet above the site, while I ran the Sky Timer.

The Sky Timer was a simple computer that measured the time it took to cover the distance of 1,320 feet (1/4 of a mile) and converted those two knowns into miles per hour. Unlike a radar reading that immediately gives you the speed at any given instant, this computed the average speed over the entire distance. The timer was started right before the vehicle's front bumper entered the section and was stopped after its rear bumper left it. By giving the violator two full car lengths, it gave the benefit of any doubt to the violator. My clocks of the patrol cars matched the predetermined speeds, and I became a certified Air Observer.

Working the plane was a lot of fun. Like going on a field trip in grade school, it was a break from normal activities for both the observer and the troopers on the ground who stopped the cars and issued the citations. Speeding vehicles were quite apparent and easy to spot a mile or two before the site. After obtaining the vehicle's speed, I would radio to the ground units, who were on the freeway on-ramp BS'ing and patiently waiting. I wore a radio headset so the pilot and I could talk, and I would depress a pedal under my foot to speak to the troopers on the ground.

"Next available ground unit, Air One," I would say.

The first trooper in line would answer by giving their NHP ID number, "6372."

"6372, you have clock number fifty-seven at eighty-seven miles per hour. It is a red sedan passing your location right now."

I would watch from the air as the ground unit would pull out, catch up to the vehicle, and confirm with me the correct vehicle, the clock number of the day, and the speed. The red lights would come as we began turning back to the site in search of another. It was like shooting fish in a barrel.

Earlier, I mentioned the dreaded and common malady, air sickness. Flying in tight circles five hundred feet above the highway for four hours straight while watching moving traffic below and working the Sky Timer system was a major "barfer." Air observers who filled the little air sickness bags located in the back of the pilot's seat every time they went up had very short careers. There is nothing fun about tossing your cookies in the back of an airplane, nor is the pilot eager for you to return. Lucky for me, I never suffered from motion sickness in my life, so I ended up with hundreds of hours in the air.

Being a ground unit was also fun. We would sit and talk with our coworkers on the side of the highway until we were called to make a stop. When we did make a stop, there was typically little argument from the violator when we informed them that they were caught speeding by the aircraft and that we were simply the ticket writer. Any future appearance in court would include the trooper in the plane who checked their speed, not the ground unit.

One day as sergeant, I was working as a ground unit on US 395 north of Reno with three other troopers. We had written several citations each when suddenly there was no more radio traffic from Air One. All four of us had gathered on the ramp and watched as the airplane left the site and became a small dot in the sky flying off to the north. Uh oh! When Air One stopped flying in circles and flew off in a straight line, it was usually a sign that the poor goose in the backseat was getting ready to barf, and we weren't disappointed.

The four of us were standing outside of our patrol cars, patiently waiting for our airplane to return, when suddenly we heard a horrendous sound over all our car and handheld radios. It wasn't enough that the poor observer was blowing chunks in the back of the airplane. Oh no, every time he leaned over to barf, his foot would hit the transmit pedal, and the event was shared with the entire group. A group of cops would find this most amusing, and we did.

In addition to catching speeders, the plane came in handy for emergency transportation of medical supplies. Nevada rural hospitals quite often found themselves in need of blood and specialized medicines like rattlesnake anti-venom. Usually, road troopers would be called to transport these items across the state. A trooper, usually in the larger cities of Reno or Las Vegas, would pick up the emergency package, and while rolling code 3 (lights and sirens), would relay it to another trooper who would move it farther and relay with another until it reached its destination. Passing these runs off to the airplane was usually faster and safer.

The airplane was also used to search for bad guys. Late one morning, NHP dispatch requested that I proceed immediately to the Humboldt County Sheriff's Office dispatch center. The dispatcher, with a smile on her face, passed me a sheet of paper with a new ATL (attempt to locate) that was just issued by the Carson City Sheriff's Office. Carson City is Nevada's capital city and home to state department headquarters, including the Highway Patrol. The Carson City Sheriff's Office was trying to find a stolen car. It was a brand-new Ford, four-door sedan, blue in color, bearing Nevada license plates, NHP001.

NHP001?

Holy cow, the chief had his car stolen!? I can't say I didn't smile at this one. Every day, I received a list of bad guys and vehicles stolen in Nevada and adjoining states, but never was the chief's car on it. Obviously, this news was not going out over the statewide NHP radio.

About mid-afternoon, after actively and silently searching for my chief's stolen patrol car, I heard radio traffic from Reno. Apparently, the NHP airplane had been searching for the chief's car from the air and had located it on a dirt road about one hundred miles north of Reno. For those of you not familiar with our state, there is nothing but dirt roads, sagebrush, and rabbits north of Reno until you hit the Oregon state line. There were no law enforcement officers or troopers within miles of there, so the pilot kept swooping down toward the car and did so enough times that the car left the road and overturned several times. The chief's car was found but had received total damage. The funny thing was when troopers finally arrived and located the driver, he had received only minor injuries in the rollover because he was wearing his seatbelt. When asked why he was wearing his seatbelt, the thief replied, "Well, it's against the law not to wear a seatbelt."

So, who stole the chief's car and why? Carson City is home to several state prisons and the Nevada Highway Patrol Academy. Several of the convicts worked as trustees at the academy and had done so for many years. They cleaned the floors, yard, classrooms, and spent a great amount of time washing cars. Any trooper who visited the academy could have their patrol car washed while there. Just give your keys to the academy staff troopers, and you had a nice shiny patrol car to drive when your business concluded.

One trustee had been a model prisoner and trustee at the academy for many years. So trustworthy, in fact, that academy staff would just toss him the keys to a patrol car, and he would move it to the wash bay and return it when finished. What made this one day different from hundreds of previous days in this model prisoner's life? Well, the night before, this inmate received a call from his longtime girlfriend who told him she was leaving him. How the heck a woman can leave a guy who has been in prison for years is a mystery to me, but the heartbreak of her dumping him was enough to cause him to steal the chief's car and head across country for his home state of Idaho.

For those of you who are still living in or visiting Nevada, there is no need to worry about getting caught speeding by the bear in the air any longer. Nevada has gotten rid of both highway patrol airplanes. Perhaps they were just too efficient.

Too Good to Be True

The old saying, "If it's too good to be true, it usually is" was quite evident one day in 1986 when I stopped a large red Chrysler four-door sedan for speeding. The vehicle was being driven by a young black man who produced an expired Texas registration, and he had no driver's license. The young man was accompanied by a younger white woman, both of whom claimed to be from Texas. Neither could produce identification, so I had no choice but to place the driver under arrest for all three violations. I had just finished handcuffing, searching, and strapping the man into my patrol car when I heard the Humboldt County Sheriff's Office dispatch center broadcast an attempt to locate (ATL) over their radio frequency.

"Attention all units. Attempt to locate two subjects, one black male and one white female, wanted in Winnemucca for Obtaining Money by False Pretenses. Last seen driving a red Chrysler four-door sedan with Texas registration. Subjects sold two video cassette recorders (VCRs) wrapped in boxes to residents that when opened were found to contain red bricks wrapped in newspaper."

I already had Reginald B. Simms, aged thirty-two years, under arrest. All I had left to do was handcuff the woman, Christy Shaffer, aged twenty-six, tell the sheriff's office I'd found their culprits, and then impound the Chrysler and have it towed to town.

"Bingo! A double hitter!" I exclaimed.

Anytime a person is taken into custody and separated from their vehicle, an Impound and Inventory Form was required to be

76

completed. While completing the form, I located fifteen VCR boxes in the trunk, all with professional images of VCRs on the front and back and pre-wrapped in factory-style cellophane. The VCR packages looked so nice that anyone looking at them would have thought that they came right out of Best Buy.

I booked the two scammers into the county jail and wasn't quite sure who I felt sorriest for, the young thieves down on their luck who desperately needed cash or the local business owners who thought they were cutting a fat hog in the rump by buying two obviously stolen VCRs out of the back of a car in broad daylight.

It is a crime for any person to knowingly receive or possess stolen property:

(a) Knowing that it is stolen property; or

(b) Under such circumstances as should have caused a reasonable person to know that it is stolen property.

I caught and booked these two crooks from Texas and never knew the outcome of the case or what sentence they received, but since it was two local business owners who paid cash for boxes of worthless red bricks, I'm sure the only thing they had to worry about was being embarrassed.

Our Days in Baker, Nevada

In far east-central Nevada lies the little town of Baker. Seventy-six miles southeast of Ely and eight miles from the western Utah border, Baker is located five miles east of the main entrance to Great Basin National Park. The town is named after an early settler, George W. Baker. According to the 2010 and 2020 census, the population of Baker stood at sixty-eight and forty-one residents respectively.

Great Basin National Park, comprising over 77,000 acres, was first set aside by President Ronald Reagan and was dedicated as such on August 16, 1987. The park is as remote as it is beautiful, with rugged mountains carved out by immense glaciers, alpine forests, extensive underground caverns, and running streams.

Numerous state and federal dignitaries, including United States senators, congressmen, governors from Nevada (present and past) and from neighboring states were scheduled to attend the dedication ceremony. I was one of a dozen state troopers assigned to work on the event, and our job was to provide armed security, direct traffic, and ensure that everyone attending arrived and departed safely.

Trooper Doug Darlington and I found ourselves assigned to direct traffic control at the only major intersection in downtown Baker. Boring is too kind of a word to use to describe our day, however, our good friend Trooper Dave Black had what turned out to be a much more difficult task.

Dave's job for the day was to work traffic control and parking at the site of the ceremony. The area chosen for the dedication ceremony was a small area beside the highway cleared of sagebrush and barely large enough to accommodate a few portable bleachers and limited parking. All vehicles arriving for the event were stopped at the entrance to the dedication clearing where Dave was to ascertain whether the vehicle was transporting any VIPs. Vehicles containing VIPs were allowed to park near the bleachers, while non-VIPs in all other vehicles were directed to continue down the highway where they could park on the side of the road and walk back. This resulted in some long walks for non-important attendees, especially latecomers.

A very nice car pulled up with three older people in it, and Trooper Black asked the male driver if he was a VIP.

The man stated, "No, young man. I am not."

"Very good, sir. Please continue down the road until you can find a place to park, and you and your guests will have to walk back."

"Very well," the man said. "However, you should know that the man in the car behind me is a United States senator."

Dave thanked the man for the information and sent him down the highway.

Dave was a Nevada boy, born and raised, and how he didn't recognize the self-proclaimed non-VIP was a mystery. This man who didn't want special treatment and who did not take the opportunity to proclaim his importance as a VIP had served eight years as the most popular governor in Nevada's history, winning his bid for reelection in 1975 by a four-to-one margin.

Oh, but the story got better. You see, Governor Donal Neil "Mike" O'Callaghan didn't just walk a couple hundred yards down the two-lane highway to the event—no, he limped. As a young man, O'Callaghan lied about his age, and at sixteen, he joined the United States Marines, serving from 1946 to 1948. After leaving the Marines, he attended college in Boise, Idaho and then joined the Air Force in 1950, serving two years as an intelligence officer in the Aleutian Islands. In 1952,

O'Callaghan was transferred to the U.S. Army where he served in the Korean War, losing his left leg to a mortar round.

Several VIPs at the event were incensed that our past governor had to walk several hundred yards with his wooden leg, which caused our upper-level commanders to sweat bullets and apologize profusely to their boss, the current governor. Trooper Black received an undeserved butt chewing, which being the good friends that we were, we found quite funny. We also realized that our past governor was popular for a reason. Unlike most politicians, Governor Mike O'Callaghan didn't think he was anything special, and those of us close to the bottom rung of the ladder appreciated that.

The other story of the dedication weekend we found amusing was a traffic stop made by Sergeant Glen Jewett where he stopped a California man for speeding and issued him a citation. Sergeant Jewett explained the citation to the very unhappy man, stating, "You have been cited for speeding. You can take care of the citation by mail as indicated in the instructions on the backside of your copy, or if you wish to appear in court, your appearance date is September 4th at 10:00 a.m. in Baker Justice Court, Baker, Nevada."

The very unhappy driver demanded that Sgt. Jewett immediately take him to see the judge, to which Sgt. Jewett replied, "Sir, that is not possible. It is Sunday, and Judge Baker is not available."

Baker Justice Court, Baker, Nevada, and Judge Baker were just too much for the poor defeated man who said, "Never mind. I'll just pay it."

In conclusion, Great Basin National Park was established, no one died, our aging ex-governor got some exercise, we laughed at our good friend Trooper Black's expense, and a good time was had by all.

Critical Speed of a Curve

How many times have you taken a curve in the road too fast? There was a yellow warning sign showing the upcoming curve, and quite often an accompanying sign suggesting a safe speed at which to take the curve, but today for some reason you didn't pay attention.

As you're entering the curve and starting to make the ever so slight turning movement of the steering wheel to negotiate the curve, you're starting to figure out that something is wrong. What's wrong? Well, you want the car to turn, but your car wants to go straight. Without getting too deep into physics or Newton's laws of motion, we will simply say that with regard to a car or truck, the faster you accelerate into a curve, the more your vehicle is pulled in the original direction by something called centrifugal force. As the centrifugal force acting on your car increases, the arc of your turn becomes wider. As you steer your car in an effort to keep it on the road and centrifugal force tries to keep your car going straight, the car begins to roll up onto the outer edge of the tires closest to the curve. This described action leaves a very distinct and identifiable mark on the roadway that is called a sideslip, a yaw scuff mark, or critical-speed scuff marks. It is made by a tire that is rotating and sliding sideways and is easily identifiable as a curved, narrow, black mark with darker black stripes across it called striations. The direction of the striations across the yaw mark tell an investigator if the vehicle was increasing, decreasing, or maintaining its speed as it left the mark.

Most often, the curved yaw mark follows the outer edge of the paved roadway and does not result in an accident. You simply remove the seat cushion from your rear end, remind yourself to slow down next time, and continue merrily down the highway. But there are those times when the speed of the vehicle surpasses the "critical speed of the curve." When this happens, the yaw mark continues to the edge of the pavement, where it ends and the rest of the accident begins, whatever that might be. With a couple of simple measurements entered into an algebraic formula, that yaw mark will supply the investigator with the minimum speed that the vehicle was traveling when it left the mark on the pavement.

I spent many weeks teaching courses of Basic, Advanced, and Technical Accident Investigation and a two-week course in Vehicle Dynamics which included close to forty algebraic formulas used to determine the velocity of a vehicle. Depending on the actions of the crash vehicle, different formulas and inputs were required, i.e. was it skidding, scuffing, rolling across the desert, going over a cliff, etc. This was meant to give academy cadets a taste of how deeply they can go into the science of Accident Investigation, and we would teach them a few very basic formulas to pique their interest. The yaw mark formula is one of the easier to learn and apply, so it was always covered.

After teaching a three-week basic accident investigation course at the academy, I returned home to Winnemucca where I would continue my duties as a trooper and accident reconstruction expert. When the cadets graduated, I was given the assignment of training a newly assigned trooper to our area. His name was Dan Hammill.

One morning, we were sent to a serious injury accident near the tiny, remote burg of Beowawe, where the speed limit decreases from fifty-five to thirty-five. We arrived at the accident scene and observed a large, older Cadillac which had left the highway somewhere close to the beginning of a long, sweeping curve. The Cadillac had extensive rollover damage, and the driver, who was reportedly intoxicated and severely injured, had been transported to the hospital in Elko before our arrival.

As Trooper Hammill and I walked through the accident scene, there it was—a classic, textbook yaw mark. Always initiated from steering, it began as a faint curve and quickly progressed into a beautifully curved, dark, thin, scuff mark with darker, zebra-stripe striations perpendicular to the mark. It was a beauty!

"Trooper Hammill, can you tell me what type of tire mark this is?" I asked.

"It looks like a yaw mark," he said.

"Hallelujah. You did learn something. But this isn't just a yaw mark, Trooper Hammill. This is the perfect yaw mark, and what are we going to do with it?"

"We are going to use it to find out how fast this guy was going."

"Yes, we are."

In order to come up with the speed, we first needed to determine the radius of the curve of the yaw mark. This was done by obtaining two measurements. The chord, which is the distance of a straight line between two points on the curve, and the middle ordinate, which is the distance of a straight line from the mid-point of the chord to the outer edge of the yaw mark. These two factors are entered into an algebraic formula, and the result is the radius of the curve of the yaw mark. The radius result, along with a number representing the drag factor (which is a measurement of the slipperiness of the roadway surface) were entered into another formula, and that gave us the minimum speed the Cadillac was going in order to leave that particular tire mark.

So, after applying some of the knowledge Trooper Hammill had gained in basic accident investigation, he was able to charge the driver with driving under the influence of alcohol, not wearing a seatbelt, and speeding 78 mph in a 35-mph speed zone.

You see, math can be fun, and people really do use algebra after they graduate from high school.

Hot-Footed Pedestrian

While summers in the high deserts of northern Nevada are nowhere near as hot as those in the south (Las Vegas), the temperature can regularly rise above 100 degrees in both July and August. On one of these hot summer days, I was notified of a man walking eastbound in the travel lane of I-80 four miles east of Winnemucca. Pedestrians should walk along the outside edge of the paved shoulder or in the dirt alongside the paved portion of the roadway to avoid traffic. Walking in or anywhere close to a travel lane meant for vehicular travel can rapidly transform a human being into an angel, so I wasted no time in getting there.

When I arrived, I saw a poorly dressed, barefoot, middle-aged man walking on the painted white line along the outside travel lane dangerously close to traffic. The man had no shoes or socks and was purposely walking on the cooler painted white line to avoid burning his feet.

The man did have water, but little else. I retrieved his identification, checked for wants and warrants, patted him down for weapons, then gave him a seat in my patrol car. It didn't matter why the man had no shoes or socks, but it was clear that he couldn't continue his journey without them. I spent the next two hours quietly taking care of the situation, but somehow Joyce Sheen, the owner and reporter of our local Winnemucca radio station, learned of my exploits and broadcast this story on the news the following day:

KWNA Radio
Monday, August 7, 1986

Many people have a stereotyped image of law enforcement personnel, and often it is not positive.

You know how it is when you're traveling down Interstate 80, and that blue car with gold stripes and flashing lights pulls up behind you. You swallow hard and start looking for your driver's license, registration, and proof of insurance, and you hope, you really hope, that you weren't going too much faster than you should have been.

Well, believe it or not, the highway patrol troopers in our small community of Winnemucca do have hearts, or at least one of them does.

It seems our state trooper spotted a barefoot fellow walking down Interstate 80 during one of our recent horridly hot days. The fellow was walking on the painted white line because it was cooler than anywhere else on the road.

The trooper radioed into the local highway patrol office and asked the secretary to check with Poke and Peek, our local thrift store, to see if they had any shoes up there, but it was not open.

The trooper radioed back that he would bring the man into town, drop him off to go to his own house, and get the walker a pair of shoes. Before long, the fellow had resumed his quest with an old pair of tennis shoes on his feet.

Who was the local trooper who did this? Well, we'll let him remain anonymous. We wouldn't want to ruin his image completely.

State troopers often interact with people when they are not at their best. Citations, arrests, and accidents are daily occurrences, so events where we can assist those in need are welcomed.

Who Was at Fault?

US 50 ("The Loneliest Highway in America") crosses seventeen different mountain passes over 409 miles of central Nevada from the California state line at South Lake Tahoe in the west to the Utah state line near Great Basin National Park in the east. Many of these ascents and descents over the mountain passes are comprised of tight, hairpin turns and steep 8% grades through pine forests, at altitudes up to 7,000 feet. The first 100 miles of US 50 passes through five Nevada towns, while the last 309 miles of it passes through three small towns, making it live up to its name.

On July 24, 1990, at approximately 3:50 p.m. on US 50, 11.2 miles east of the small town of Austin, Nevada, a head-on accident occurred between two vehicles, a Datsun two-door sedan and a Toyota four-door sedan. The Datsun (driven by a man) was attempting to enter the highway from a large, dirt parking area on the south side of the road. The Toyota (driven by a woman) was traveling eastbound down Austin Summit on a left-hand, slight downhill curve bordered by a guardrail. The Datsun pulled onto the highway to head west directly in front of the eastbound Toyota. The driver of the Toyota hit the brakes, and the Datsun made it to the westbound side of the highway, where the Toyota, sliding in a locked-wheel skid, crossed over the centerline, into the westbound lane, and struck the Datsun in the driver's door, killing the man.

The trooper, who resided in the small town of Austin, was

actually very good at investigating motor vehicle accidents, but after submitting his report, I was called in as a reconstruction expert to look at the dynamics of the crash and either confirm or dispute the trooper's findings of fault. Because the Datsun was on its proper side of the highway when it was struck, and the Toyota had crossed over the centerline before striking the Datsun and killing the driver, the trooper listed the driver of the Toyota as at fault.

I arrived at the accident scene one week later on July 31st and began my work. The first step in any accident reconstruction is to determine what relevant questions need to be asked and answered to determine fault. Was the driver of the eastbound Toyota traveling so fast that the other driver couldn't have seen it before he pulled out? If not, why didn't the driver of the Datsun see the Toyota? Why didn't the Toyota stay on its side of the highway? Had the driver of the Toyota not locked up the brakes and stayed on her side of the highway, would the accident have occurred at all? Essentially, I needed to determine the speeds of each vehicle involved and which, of any violations that occurred, was the primary cause of the accident.

There were locked-wheel skid marks from the Toyota which crossed the centerline of the highway and terminated where the two vehicles collided. Four collision scrub marks (one from each tire) were located at the same area and were left by the tires of the Datsun. The collision scrub marks were not parallel to the travel lane, proving that the Datsun was still completing its left turn when it was struck.

As far as determining the speed of each vehicle at impact, there were locked-wheel skid marks left by the Toyota prior to impact. These were straight, with no rotation, indicating even braking. The left side locked first, the skid marks crossing over the centerline approximately three and a half feet before collision. No tire marks were located from the Datsun prior to impact. Both vehicles, after collision and maximum engagement, separated and moved away from each other. Each vehicle left post-impact tire marks from the point of collision until position of final rest.

Newton's third law of motion states that, "For every action (force) in nature, there is an equal and opposite reaction." Without going into too much detail, this law of motion means that the energy after the impact would be equal and opposite to the energy before impact. As reconstruction experts, we were taught to apply a principle called the "Conservation of Momentum." By determining the post-impact velocities and knowing the weight of each vehicle, I could determine the approximate velocity (FPS or feet per second) of each vehicle prior to impact. The result can be determined mathematically or by drawing a parallelogram. The velocity of the Toyota at impact was 70.4 FPS or 48 miles per hour. The energy lost by skidding put the vehicle's initial speed, before it started braking, at 61 miles per hour. The velocity of the Datsun at impact was 18.47 FPS or 12 miles per hour.

My calculations demonstrated that the Toyota was not traveling at an excessive speed and was in a position to be visible to the driver of the Datsun when he started his turn and entered the highway. The low-profile design of the Datsun and the presence of the guardrail were both enough to obscure the driver's view of approaching traffic.

The roadway had a negative (downhill) grade of -.01. More importantly, the highway had a negative super-elevation (the amount by which the outer edge of a curve on a road is banked above the inner edge) of -.08. When a vehicle's brakes are locked and the vehicle is sliding on the roadway, it is always going to slide downhill. This meant that when the Datsun pulled onto the highway, directly into the path of the Toyota, and the woman hit the brakes to avoid striking the Datsun, it was physically impossible for the Toyota to not slide downhill across the centerline. Had the driver of the Toyota not hit the brakes, her vehicle would have continued at its same velocity and the accident would have still occurred. Therefore, the accident-causing violation was "Failure to yield to oncoming traffic" by the driver of the Datsun and not "Driving left of center" by the driver of the Toyota as the trooper had originally listed.

I tried like hell to explain this to the investigating trooper, but he was just as stubborn as they come. I submitted my report to the lieutenant and never knew if the original report was amended. Hopefully it was, and the woman didn't have to live her life believing she had killed another person, because she was not at fault for that accident.

The Rainbow Family Gathering

In mid-June 1989, I received orders to work the annual "Rainbow Family Gathering," scheduled to be held July 1st to the 7th at Robinson Hole in the remote area of northeastern Nevada. Permit me to explain a little bit about this event, as I previously had no idea such a group existed. The "Rainbow Family" is a loose-knit group of counterculture warriors, many left over from the sixties. Also known as the "Rainbow Family Tribe," they are a collection of old hippies, aging flower children, free spirits, and children of humankind willing to protest every evil cause known to modern man. Every year during the first week of July, the group (sometimes numbering in the tens of thousands) invades a National Forest somewhere in America. At the end of each event, they select the next year's gathering site, and in July 1988, someone in the group chose Robinson Hole.

Robinson Hole is a deep canyon in the middle of the Humboldt National Forest in the extreme northern end of Elko County, seven miles south of the Idaho border. It is an extremely beautiful and wild area made up of high desert plateaus with an elevation of 6,000 feet separated by deep canyons that can steeply drop a thousand feet or more. I have described many places in my home state of Nevada as remote, but Robinson Hole makes those places look handy. It is so far out that the jackrabbits carry canteens. It is a difficult and sometimes impossible drive certain times of the year. These flower children, most of whom are city-dwellers, were in for quite a surprise!

I was one of ten state troopers assigned to assist the Elko County

Sheriff's Office, which was responsible for the attendees' safety during this event. The Rainbow Family were known to indulge in illegal drugs, and during that week, everything from black tar heroin and LSD to meth and weed was confiscated, but very few arrests were made. It was just too darn far from jail and too rough of a road to get them there. And there was a larger problem far beyond thousands of urban folks camping and using drugs at the bottom of Robinson Hole, and that was fire. Both the state of Nevada and the federal government had numerous wildland fire crews on site with absolutely nothing to do unless a fire broke out. Had a fire started, there would not have been enough manpower. Hundreds of dollars' worth of 4th of July fireworks were confiscated from the urban-dwelling flower children who did not realize that fireworks of any kind were illegal in Nevada and that any fire in the area could most certainly contribute to their own demise. With the deep canyon being accessible by only one steep long trail, if any kind of serious brush fire started, it would most likely result in the loss of life.

The ten troopers assigned to the event stayed in the little remote town of Jarbidge, Nevada. I happened to have a lifelong friend who owned a very nice cabin in Jarbidge, so I and two of my closest friends stayed in comparable luxury while the rest of the crew slept in the barracks at Mahoney Ranger Station. As the crow flies, Jarbidge is only seven miles from Robinson Hole, but the Jarbidge Mountains (which rise to 10,800 feet in elevation) lie directly in between, so the trip was forty miles of road, most of it comprised of dirt and within the state of Idaho where we had no jurisdiction.

The week started with a briefing by our highway patrol captain and lieutenant who arrived at the Mahoney Ranger Station after a five-and-a-half-hour drive from our regional headquarters in Elko. All the troopers assigned to this event were Nevada boys, and we were excited to be there. While at work, we were getting paid to cruise our Nevada mountains in four-wheel drive patrol cars and hunt for dope. When off-duty, we were looking forward to a fun week flyfishing for trout in the Jarbidge River and drinking a few beers at the Outdoor Inn, the only small bar and restaurant within half a day's drive. Leave it to a captain and lieutenant to ruin a good time.

Captain White addressed the group. "Gentlemen, there will be absolutely no drinking this next week, and you are to keep your portable radios with you at all times while off-duty. Short of the crime of murder, you are not to arrest anybody. Your job is to patrol in two-man units and get the hippies safely from point A (the edge of civilization) to point B (Robinson Hole) and back."

After completing his diatribe on numerous other topics, the captain and lieutenant got in their patrol car and pulled out of the Mahoney Ranger Station on the dirt road, leaving a big cloud of dust. Before the dust settled, the troopers from Elko asked, "You guys want a beer?"

"You have beer?" I asked.

"Heck yes, we do, and this event doesn't officially start until tomorrow, which means we had better get rid of it today."

Two troopers walked across the yard to a large well casing, took off the lid, and pulled up a rope that had numerous six-packs tied to it. We had a good time that night visiting together and laughing, but unfortunately that was the last of the beer.

Being tied to a radio and having to respond if called was nothing new, but carrying it while flyfishing in the Jarbidge River was worrisome. One slip or fall resulting in a drowned and ruined radio meant big trouble and several memos.

As far as work was concerned, we did exactly what we were told to do. My partner was my longtime friend and fellow trooper from Winnemucca, Dave Black. We worked from 4:00 p.m. until midnight and helped the rainbow people as they traversed across the high desert and mountain roads. We collected and confiscated more drugs than we had seen in months and did so without arresting a soul. We played cribbage on the console while enjoying the many jalopies, vans, and painted buses moving about the desert.

Late one night, well past dark, we were in Idaho about one mile north of the Nevada state line when we came upon a dozen or so people standing outside of their vehicles passing around a couple of marijuana joints.

I was driving, and we were approaching from the north, so I told Dave, "When I say, 'now,' turn on the overhead (red and blue) lights."

When we got close, I said, "Now."

Dave flipped on the overheads, and the joints flew like fireflies from fingertips into the dirt. We stopped immediately, and trying our best not to laugh, we asked the group, "Do you folks have any weed on you?"

"No, sir," was the reply from the chorus.

"Well, that's a good thing," I replied. "Because the Nevada border is just ahead of you, and any amount of marijuana in Nevada, even one seed, is a felony!"

Remember this was 1989, and at the time Nevada had some of the toughest drug laws in the nation.

"One seed is a felony?" a guy asked.

"Yes, it is," I said.

"Well, we don't have any illegal drugs with us," cried the chorus.

"That's good," Dave said. "We're Nevada troopers, and because we are in Idaho, there's nothing we could do anyway. But once you cross that state line, you're fair game."

"How far is the state line?" one asked.

"About one mile," said Dave.

"How will we know when we get there? Is it clearly marked?"

Dave said, "This is a remote dirt road, and normally it is not, but this week it is. Have a good night!"

We laughed as we drove away from a group of very polite young people who were now in a quandary as to what to do with a supply of drugs that they claimed they didn't have.

There was some dissension in the crowd that week. While many of the attendees were choking down the community soup (a giant pot filled with the contributions of whoever walked by and threw something in it), the administrators of the group were miles away at Murphy's Hot Springs Resort soaking in the tubs and eating steak on family funds. Word of the leaders spending Rainbow Family funds on lavish meals and hot tubs spread faster than the wildfire that never happened.

In Robinson Hole, nudity was rampant, love was made, a lot of dope was consumed, and the Rainbow Family had a wonderful time. As for us troopers, we ate well, had fun at work, and burned up a bunch of Nevada's gas cruising the deserts and mountains we called home. We even caught and released lots of fish, and luckily the radios survived. Overall, the 1989 Rainbow Family Gathering was a success.

Nevada F.A.R.T.

In the mid-1980s, the Nevada Highway Patrol sent their first group of troopers to Northwestern University in Evansville, Illinois to be trained as accident reconstruction experts. This group returned from this very difficult and extensive training and brought our department's accident investigation responsibilities to a new level. Serious vehicle accidents resulting in felony prosecutions or lawsuits resulting in millions of dollars were often reviewed by professional engineers who were trained and paid to either dispute our conclusions as to what occurred or to cast doubt on our findings in court, making it difficult to get a conviction. As a result, training troopers as accident reconstruction experts who could compete with college-educated professionals became a necessity. The big equalizer turned out to be experience. While engineers sat in classrooms learning theory and dynamics, troopers were handling wreck after wreck, gaining actual experience in vehicle dynamics.

Most of the Nevada Highway Patrol's first accident reconstruction experts worked as individuals. It wasn't until the larger second group (of which I was a part) was trained that the department began to consider having us work together as a team so that we could draw upon each other's knowledge and experience. Many serious accidents often require more than one expert, and by working together, there would be less room for error and we could get to a conclusion on high-profile accidents quicker by checking and double-checking each other's application of reconstruction principles.

Accident reconstruction is not an exact science. Most everything is based on approximates, and sometimes conclusions can be reached using different methods. One of my instructors, Thaddeus Alcock from Northwestern University, was raised in central North Carolina and spoke with a distinctive southern drawl. His favorite saying was, "In accident reconstruction, two plus two ain't necessarily f*#king four!"

Though our state is the seventh-largest in size, it has one of the smallest state police agencies in the nation. Therefore, everyone knew everyone, and it wasn't uncommon to see our colonel (chief) regularly and to be able to meet with him. He was all for having a team concept when it came to accident reconstruction and asked us if we had any ideas for a name. California called theirs M.A.I.T. for Major Accident Investigation Team, so we couldn't possibly use that name. Instead, we came up with Nevada Highway Patrol F.A.R.T. for Fatal Accident Reconstruction Team.

While laughing about the name we were sure the colonel wouldn't go for, we came up with slogans we could put on t-shirts beneath the new F.A.R.T. logo.

Mine would read: "Don't wear your seatbelt. I need the overtime!"

Others examples my teammates came up with were:

"Low IQ + High Testosterone + Alcohol = Job Security!"

"We are only one car crash away from death!"

"When your lights go out, ours come on!"

Our colonel had a good sense of humor but just didn't think Nevada F.A.R.T. was going to work, so we left off the F and were known simply as the Accident Reconstruction Team.

Oh well, we tried!

That's Your Job

July 1, 1987, Nevada passed the first law requiring the use of seatbelts. In order to make the new law more palatable to Nevada drivers, it was declared a secondary violation, meaning a driver had to be pulled over for another reason before a seatbelt violation could be charged.

Not long after came child seat laws based on age, weight, front seat vs. backseat, and facing forward vs. facing backward. These new laws were confusing for most people, but certainly important and necessary for child safety.

One afternoon, I worked an accident on I-80 at the top of Golconda Summit where an infant, who was strapped into a car seat, was ejected (seat and all) from the vehicle. The package tumbled down the roadway with the child receiving only minor injuries. The seat was not properly strapped inside the vehicle but still saved the baby's life when it came flying out of the car.

Since the child seat law was still new, we were issuing more warnings than citations at the time. One day on I-80 near Button Point, I was passed by an old beat-up station wagon driven by a lone woman with the back of the car filled with kids. I counted five little munchkins jumping over seats, standing up, and pushing each other. Though I couldn't hear it, they appeared to be laughing and screaming. The driver must have known that the rodeo in the rear of her car was not allowed because I could see a look of concern on her face as she did her best to ignore me. I had seen this car before, so I knew she lived in Winnemucca. I pulled the stressed-out lady over, and as close to tears as she was, I could tell she was near the end of her rope.

"Ma'am, I am Trooper Raabe with the Nevada Highway Patrol. I have stopped you today because you cannot have small children running around the back of your car as you drive. Are you familiar with the child safety laws recently passed requiring that all young children be in safety seats?"

"I have heard of it, but I don't really understand it," she replied.

"Well, even if you don't understand the new laws concerning safety seats for children, you must know that seatbelts have been required for quite some time. At the very least, they should be sitting down with seatbelts on!"

"Yes," she stated. "I try to strap them in, but they just get out of them, and when I tell them to put them back on, they don't listen to me."

"Ma'am, if these children won't listen to you at this young age, they certainly won't listen to you when they're teenagers."

"Officer," she asked, "would you tell them that they need to stay seated with their seatbelts on?"

"No, ma'am," I replied. "I will not. It's my job to tell you. It's your job to tell them and make them listen."

"They don't listen to me," she repeated.

"Have you tried a stick?" I asked.

The lady reached under the seat and pulled out a lightweight paint mixing stick, the kind they give you when you buy a gallon of paint and asked, "Like this?"

I smiled and said, "Well, that's a start. I've seen you around before, so I will be watching to see that these children are strapped in properly. This warning is on me. If there is a next violation, it's on you, and it's a large fine."

When the woman drove off, the children were seated and strapped in. I have seen many children hurt and killed in traffic accidents.

Whether you are a believer in parental corporal punishment or not, I guarantee you a sore butt is a lot better than the injuries or death that result from being ejected from a moving vehicle.

The Leg Is Broken

I was at my son's junior soccer game one Saturday morning when I watched Tim collide violently with another player and fall to the ground holding his shin. As a state trooper and EMT, I had seen my share of busted bones and was afraid he'd broken his leg. Tim didn't shed a tear, but the pain was obvious.

I carried Tim to our family van and drove down the street to Humboldt General Hospital in Winnemucca. The doctor on duty ordered an X-ray and confirmed that Tim's leg was indeed broken. Three days later, we met with an orthopedic surgeon in Reno. He looked at the X-ray and decided that surgery was unnecessary. Tim's leg was placed in a cast, and we returned home to Winnemucca.

Several months had passed when I received a bill from an unfamiliar radiologist in Reno. Apparently, the doctor had commuted from Reno to read Tim's X-rays and charged me $160 for the service. I called the billing office and asked why it was necessary for the radiologist to read the X-ray after Tim's leg was already in a cast. I was told that state law required a radiologist to read all X-rays and I asked for a copy of the law. The story then changed. Review of X-rays by a radiologist wasn't a law, but a requirement relating to hospital accreditation.

The money wasn't as big of an issue to me as the principle. If the doctor had read the X-ray and consulted with the surgeon before he fixed the leg, I would have paid the bill. Reading the X-ray after the leg was in a cast seemed the ultimate racket. I continued to receive bills for several months. I called the doctor's office multiple times and told them to quit sending the bill. I wasn't going to pay it. The bills stopped, the leg healed, and we carried on with life.

Two years later, a major storm blew into northern Nevada. I-80 west of the Mill City Interchange was a sheet of ice with blowing snow. Two men were in my patrol car, and I was completing paperwork on accident number four of the day. The man next to me in the front seat was the driver. He'd lost control of their Chevy suburban on the ice-covered roadway. The suburban landed upside down in the center median of the interstate.

My patrol car was parked just off the road on the westbound side of the median. While calling for a tow truck, one of the men yelled, "Look! That car is out of control!"

I looked up and watched a car spinning out of control in the eastbound lanes. The car remained on its wheels and left the south road edge backwards into the median. After a rough ride over the steep embankment, the car stopped sixty feet from my patrol car. A woman, shaken and crying, climbed out of the damaged car. She walked the short distance to my patrol car. The man in the front seat moved to the back to make room for the driver of accident number five.

A very nice woman sat in my car and handed me her driver's license. I looked at it and recognized the name of the radiologist. I looked at her and said, "It's you, the doctor!"

The doctor looked at my name tag and still on the verge of tears said, "It's you, Trooper Raabe! We finally meet!"

Both of us busted up laughing! While waiting for two tow trucks to arrive, we had time to visit. This doctor, whose name I will never forget, was an absolute sweetheart. She could have easily become a friend. Our paths never crossed again, but I'm sure the doctor will remember the day we met as long as she lives. I know I won't forget it.

I Think You're Missing the Point

It always amazed me that in a state where alcohol is sold most anywhere at any time and flows like rivers from the doors of every casino in the state, Nevada had some of the toughest DUI laws in the nation. While Nevadans demand that law breakers be held accountable, they also have a history of trying to keep government out of our personal business. Nevada has been famous for its historic lawless stance on divorce, alcohol, gambling, and legalized prostitution. And even though we have somehow become eastern California in recent years, those of us who have spent our lives here hope the government's general hands-off approach on many issues continues.

Being arrested for driving while intoxicated brings a multitude of expensive, embarrassing, and inconvenient realities into one's life. From jail, attorneys, tow bills, and trials to suspended driver's licenses, higher insurance costs, and having to attend DUI school, it's nothing anyone would choose to do, yet every day new participants are arrested, and the process continues.

As a state trooper, I was well-versed in all aspects of DUI detection, enforcement, and prosecution, but I never had anything to do with post-conviction follow-up which included probation, community service, victim-impact panels, ignition interlock devices on cars, and passing a state-certified course on driving under the influence.

Since raising a family on a trooper's salary always seemed to leave me short of funds on payday, I applied to the Department of Motor Vehicles to open my own DUI school in my small town of

Winnemucca. I submitted a prepared lesson plan and all the required documents to the state and received a reply that arresting DUIs and then having them pay me to go to my school was a conflict of interest. I hadn't thought of that before, but it made sense, so I took another route.

I had a good friend, Laura Hummel, who was very active in Alcoholics Anonymous and other drug and alcohol rehab programs, so I approached her about owning the DUI school where I would teach the classes. Laura agreed, and before long our DUI school was approved. The state-mandated course was a total of eight hours in the classroom, so we scheduled our classes every Wednesday evening from eight to ten p.m. for four weeks and waited for our first customers.

Before long, the Winnemucca Justice Court forwarded the names of our first DUI course attendees, four in total, all of whom had been provided with instructions on when and where to show up for class. I taught several different subjects throughout my career and enjoyed it, so I was eager to get started.

The first night of school, my four students arrived together, which seemed odd. But that turned out to be the least of my concerns. I knew in advance that each of my students had Latino surnames, but it never dawned on me that none of them would be conversant in English—three spoke none, and one barely. I had previously attended a two-week course called "Spanish for Police Officers," and I was very good at saying things like "Drop the weapon... You're under arrest... Is this your car?" and "What was the missing child wearing when you last saw him?" That was about the extent of my Spanish, so I explained to the one man who spoke a little English that the class would be canceled for the night and that they would be required to arrange for an interpreter to accompany them to class the following week.

The next week, my four Latino students all arrived at the same time together with one interpreter, and the class began. At the first break, while conversing with all of them, I asked the interpreter which one of the men he knew, and he said that he knew all four men. Then I asked the interpreter about the arrangements the four men made with him to pay for his services.

The interpreter answered, "Beer!"

"Beer?" I asked.

"Yes, beer," stated the man. "Every week, they are to give me two cases of beer."

The interpreter conveyed my questions and his answers to the group, and all of us began to laugh.

"I think that all of you are missing the point," I said. "But as far as I know there are no rules regarding the compensation of interpreters, so I guess cases of beer works."

I had a lot of fun with that group over the next four weeks, and despite their agreement to pay the interpreter in cases of beer, they must have learned a thing or two because I never saw any of them in DUI school again.

Let's Take the Back Roads

As the morning sun rose high enough to reveal the details of a new day, something caught the eye of a commercial truck driver. The driver was eastbound on I-80 in northeastern Nevada, crossing the Humboldt River Bridge and approaching the Carlin Tunnels. The Carlin Tunnels were drilled through solid rock so traffic could pass directly through a mountain rather than follow the old highway route that twisted and turned along the banks of the river. It was March 17, 1991, and as the truck driver crossed the bridge and looked down towards the river, he spotted what appeared to be the body of a man wedged between two rocks on the river's edge. This sighting began the investigation of a fatal traffic accident which had resulted in the death of two brothers.

The Sunday house-warming party at the brother's friend's new house in Carlin, Nevada started at 3:00 p.m. and ended around 10:30 p.m. With plenty of food and alcohol present, everyone had a wonderful time, but now the intoxicated participants were faced with a very common problem: What to do next. Do they stay the night? Do they get picked up by someone sober? Did they think ahead and plan for a designated driver? Or, like most intoxicated human beings, did their ability to reason and make good decisions disappear as their blood-alcohol level increased and they thought they could make it home? Unfortunately for these two brothers, they chose the latter.

The discussion at the end of the party by those still present was that the brothers should spend the night. Someone actually tried to take the keys to the brothers' pickup, but that almost ended in a fight.

In their drunken condition, the brothers decided to drive home and came up with a plan to not get caught. They decided to take old US 40 back to their home in Elko rather than the much busier and more often patrolled I-80.

Old US 40, also known as the Lincoln Highway, was America's first national memorial to President Abraham Lincoln. It was also one of the first transcontinental highways built for automobiles. US 40 was dedicated on October 31 (Nevada Day), 1913 and ran from Times Square in New York City to Lincoln Park in San Francisco. In the 1970s, US 40 was replaced by I-80, a more modern highway which paralleled much of US 40 through northern Nevada. Parts of old US 40 across Nevada became secondary highways and interstate frontage roads, while the rest of it was removed.

The portion of US 40 (also known as Chestnut Street) which the brothers attempted to take home runs east from Carlin to Elko and is a two-lane, two-directional highway that runs straight for several miles before making a sharp, ninety-degree turn to the left following a tight bend in the Humboldt River. The highway then passes under both separate bridges of eastbound and westbound I-80, which span the Humboldt River just prior to entering the Carlin Tunnels. The sharp turn in the highway was well-marked with a warning sign suggesting a decreased speed limit. The south roadway edge was bordered by a steel guardrail and a barbed wire fence around the tight curve. The beginning of this sharp turn is where the accident began.

The intoxicated brothers approached this curve at a very high rate of speed, and the driver must have sensed they were in trouble because he laid down 92 feet of locked-wheel skid before their pickup truck exceeded the critical speed of the curve and began to overturn. Each traffic accident, for the purposes of reporting, has what is called the classifying event. It is the first sign of damage or injury to an object or person. As the truck overturned, the first sign of injury (or classifying event) was identified by the first of many pieces of skin left hanging on the barbed wire fence from the passenger's right arm. From that point on, this was one of the most gruesome accidents I was ever involved with. The pickup truck continued to overturn onto its right side on top of the guardrail. Neither brother was wearing a seatbelt, and the driver, now on top of his brother and pushing him through the window opening, could do nothing while his brother was being ground away beneath him by the steel and wooden posts. The truck continued rolling over onto its top as it slid onto the guardrail around a portion of the curve. The truck's left front then struck a guardrail support post, severely reducing the vehicle's forward momentum below its center of mass, causing it to rotate counterclockwise and vault over the right-of-way fence. The passenger was finally ejected at this point, followed immediately after by his brother, who came to rest fifty-four feet away at the river's edge. The truck, having landed on its wheels, rolled down the hill and into the river. The entire accident went undiscovered until observed at sunup by the commercial driver.

As a reconstruction expert, I was called the next day to examine the accident scene and answer three questions critical to the investigation. One: Which of the two brothers, Ricky or Russell, was the driver? Two: What was the critical speed, or maximum speed, at which the ninety-degree curve could be negotiated? Three: What was the minimum speed of the pickup just prior to the driver losing control?

Determining the driver was as easy as matching the skin from the barbed wire fence at the very beginning of the accident to the missing piece of skin on Ricky's right arm. Matching this and other injuries indicated that the younger brother Russell was the driver.

By taking several measurements of the curve in the roadway and entering them into an algebraic formula, the critical speed of the curve was determined to be 41 mph. The speed zone was 45 mph, with a warning sign indicating the sharp turn and an advisory speed of 25 mph.

To determine the minimum velocity (feet per second) of the pickup at the very beginning of the accident, I had to break the accident down into three different actions of the pickup. Starting at the end of the accident and working toward the beginning, I had to first look at the vault the pickup took when its left front struck the guardrail post, causing it to abruptly overturn. By measuring the difference in height from where the center of mass of the pickup took off to where it landed, as well as the distance between these two points, I could arrive at the minimum amount of velocity required for the pickup to perform this action.

Next, I had to determine the minimum amount of energy (velocity) that was lost as the pickup overturned onto, and slid on top of, the guardrail. The result was a minimum of 62.53 feet per second and did not include any energy/velocity lost to impact damage with multiple wooden guardrail posts.

Finally, I had to determine how much energy/velocity was lost by the pickup as it slid ninety-two feet down the highway prior to striking the guardrail. By knowing the distance the pickup skidded down the highway, the minimum velocity of the pickup when it first overturned onto the guardrail, and the number attributed to the drag factor (or slipperiness) of the pavement, I could calculate the minimum velocity of the pickup at the beginning of the accident to be 84.66 feet per second or 57.59 miles per hour.

Without going into numerous algebraic formulas, or exactly how all this math is used to reach very accurate results, this does give you an idea into the science of accident reconstruction.

As is too often the case, what began as a fun event resulted in the loss of two precious young lives. The friends of these two young men will never forget the chance they had to take away their keys, and their immediate family will be sad forever about the poor choices made that night.

What Are You, a Bum?

I was assigned the early Winnemucca day shift, which allowed me to get home in time to take my daughter, Corrie, and two of her fellow Brownies, Melissa and Tracy, out to sell Girl Scout cookies after school. My beautiful wife, Janelle, was the scout leader, and I had the pleasure of escorting these seven-year-old girls around downtown to state, county, and city government offices where the employees, most of whom I knew, placed large orders.

We were having a fun and successful afternoon in downtown Winnemucca until our small group reached the corner of 4th and Melarkey Streets, where we came across a homeless man seated upon a three-foot-tall concrete wall. The first transcontinental railroad passed through Winnemucca in 1868, and hobos (now referred to as homeless) have always frequented railroad towns, so running across this individual was no surprise.

As the girls and I walked past this man, he looked at me and asked, "Hey, buddy, do you have an extra dollar?"

I have always tried to show respect and be courteous to everyone, regardless of their situation, so I nicely said, "Not today, friend. I don't have any extra money."

The man raised his voice and said, "What are you an f-ing bum? You don't have any f-ing money?"

I was perturbed by this guy's language around these little girls but considered the source, so I ignored him, and we continued walking. When I became a state trooper, I made a promise to myself that I would never let a rude, obnoxious person influence my actions, and I seldom did. Most people are not at their best when they have been pulled over or are being arrested, so them being out of sorts was expected.

Suddenly, the man jumped off the wall and ran up behind my group, waving his arms and screaming obscenities. I turned around not knowing what was coming next and stood my ground between the bum and the little girls who were frightened by the sudden confrontation. I backed our small group up toward the intersection, where the four of us turned and skedaddled across the street to the unemployment office.

A good friend of mine, Marisol Guzman, was the manager there, so I opened the door, herded the girls inside, and asked her, "Marisol, would you be so kind as to keep an eye on these Brownies for a few minutes. And would you please call the police department and have an officer meet me across the street."

I left the girls, walked back across the street, and the man immediately renewed his verbal assault.

"I don't have a dollar," I said. "But I do have a place where you can spend the night and get a couple of free meals!"

We were half a block from the police department, so a Winnemucca police officer arrived within minutes. The police had received a few calls on this subject and were already on their way. I arrested the man and asked the officer to take him to booking and place him in a holding cell until I could get there to complete the paperwork.

I collected the girls, and we walked two blocks to the highway patrol office. My wife was our secretary, so I asked her to please keep an eye on the girls while I booked my bum in for the night.

Right outside the jail, I bumped into our justice court judge and district attorney who were returning from a late lunch. I relayed my story to both and was not surprised when they told me that the same man had verbally assaulted them an hour earlier.

"Well, gentlemen," I said, "this guy surprised me, and it wasn't until he chased me and my Brownies down and got right in my face that I decided to arrest him, but I am at a bit of a loss as to what to charge him with."

The judge looked at me and said, "Well, Trooper Raabe, I believe the man disturbed your peace."

"Yes, judge. You're right," I said. "That's exactly what he did. He disturbed my peace!"

"Your Honor, what is the bail for disturbing Trooper Raabe's peace today?" I asked.

The judge replied, "Five hundred dollars."

Sadly, so many of these people suffer from mental health problems, so the district attorney asked me to place a mental health hold on the man, ensuring him a visit from a mental health professional before his release.

The remainder of the cookie-selling afternoon was a bust, but at the very least the man was given a warm place to sleep, decent food, and the citizens of Winnemucca were spared his aggressive behavior for the remainder of the afternoon.

I Arrived Kicking and Screaming

Within most state police agencies, there are many different positions that troopers can be assigned to, such as traffic enforcement, commercial enforcement, K-9 handling, auto theft, and governor's security, to name a few. My first thirteen years, I was assigned to traffic enforcement where my main duties were issuing citations, assisting motorists, searching for wanted persons and fugitives, DUI detection, investigating motor vehicle accidents (with specialized training as an accident reconstruction expert), and just enough basic training in commercial vehicle enforcement to be a mild pain in the rear to experienced truck drivers. Commercial enforcement was a very specialized area that I had absolutely no interest in doing, but I was eventually dragged into it kicking and screaming.

I had three years as a trooper when I took my first promotional exam, which I did not pass. Over the next seven years, I tried two more times and passed, but not high enough to be offered a position. On my fourth attempt, with twelve years of experience working the road, I finally figured out the secret to passing the sergeant's exam high enough to be promoted. The secret that had evaded me for several years was studying. Not kind of studying, not moderately studying, but six full months with my head in the books. My wife, Janelle, grilled me regularly on all topics and would have scored high herself if given the opportunity. My longtime friend and sergeant, Doug Darlington, arranged several practice oral boards for me, using volunteer supervisors from other police departments.

When testing day arrived, I sat in highway patrol headquarters, awaiting my turn when our chief, Colonel William "Bill" Yukish, walked by and asked, "Trooper Raabe, are you ready?"

"Yes, sir," I responded. "I have never been more ready for a test in my life!"

Colonel Yukish wished me well and went on with his business.

When the test results came in, I finished number one on the statewide list and was immediately offered a traffic sergeant position in Elko, Nevada. I talked it over with Janelle and accepted the offer. The next day, we put our house up for sale, and it sold in three days. The following day, a trooper in Las Vegas, unhappy with the results, filed a grievance over the testing process. Promotions of all sergeants came to a screeching halt until the grievance worked its way through state government hearings and the courts. The Elko sergeant position was filled with a transfer, my family moved into a small rental, and we stayed in Winnemucca for a year and a half before the list was finally approved.

The day the list was approved, I received a call from Captain Mike Hood, who asked if I was interested in either of two traffic sergeant positions available in Reno. I informed him that I was, and he told me that he would call me back. Two hours later, he called and advised me that both Reno traffic sergeant positions had been filled and asked if I would be interested in a traffic sergeant position in Tonopah, a remote little town in central Nevada that I quickly and firmly rejected. Any of the top five candidates on our promotional list could be selected first to fill any position, but after a year and a half of waiting, attending court hearings, moving my family to a rental, studying so hard, finishing number one, and then being passed over for two positions first offered to me was beyond belief. Never in my career had I gotten presumptuous with any superior officer, but one and a half years of frustration had built up, so I was not at my best.

"Captain Hood, what the hell! I'm not going to Tonopah! Did you people forget who was number one on this list? Tonopah? Are you all crazy?"

Captain Hood was simply the messenger and was aware of the sergeants list from hell. He said he was sorry and that he would call me back.

An hour later, Captain Hood called back and asked, "Would you be interested in a commercial enforcement sergeant position in Reno?"

"Commercial enforcement? I'm a traffic guy. I don't do trucks!" I said. "What other choices are there right now?"

"That's it," he said.

Extremely angry for getting screwed by command and needing to get my family situated in a decent house prompted me to accept the position of commercial enforcement sergeant. So, we packed up and moved from Winnemucca, and off I went to supervise troopers in an area of enforcement I knew little about and had less interest in learning.

The Commercial Enforcement Section had only been a part of the Highway Patrol Division for about seven years before I was promoted. Prior to that time, it was known as the Motor Carrier Division whose main purpose was to collect license fees and fuel taxes on all in-state and out-of-state commercial vehicles that operated in Nevada. Their uniformed officers were known as field agents, and they attended the same academy as troopers. Field agents also enforced state laws relating to commercial vehicle safety and allowable weights on Nevada highways. In the mid-1980s, the United States Department of Transportation began contracting with individual states to enforce Federal Motor Carrier Safety Regulations. When that happened, the Nevada Highway Patrol became the division responsible for enforcement, field agents became troopers, and the commercial enforcement section was created. The United States Department of Transportation dictated and set the commercial enforcement section's responsibilities, our yearly production goals, and paid the salaries of all personnel assigned to the section.

Few citizens know about the Nevada Highway Patrol Commercial Enforcement Section or what the job entails, so I will explain. Over four million commercial vehicle safety inspections are performed every year throughout our nation to ensure that large commercial trucks and buses driving on our highways are operating safely, and Nevada troopers do their fair share. There are eight different levels of vehicle and driver inspections, which our troopers perform daily at various locations including individual Nevada trucking companies, temporary commercial vehicle check sites along our highways, and while on patrol. Many of these inspections are extensive, time-consuming, and quite thorough where the condition of every vital component is examined, even underneath. Twice each year, every school bus in the state is inspected for safety, all deficiencies are noted, and corrections are required. Commercial troopers receive extensive training in labeling requirements, shipping, the dangers involved, and the transportation of hazardous and radioactive materials. Laws regarding state registration fees, fuel taxes, and weight limits to protect the condition of our highways are still enforced.

When I showed up for work the first day, Trooper Gary Johnson, very experienced and competent in the complex and vast field of commercial vehicle safety and compliance, became my advisor and savior. It was amazing how much I didn't know, and Trooper Johnson basically babysat me until I gained the vital training and knowledge months later.

Surprisingly, and luckily for me, commercial enforcement sergeant turned out to be a great job. I worked with dedicated troopers every day, while most of the command officers had little interest in commercial enforcement and treated our section like a neglected stepchild, leaving us free to operate with no advice or interference. And it was refreshing to deal with professional truck drivers instead of angry motorists.

In 2022, 42,795 people died in traffic accidents in America, and over ten percent of those accidents involved commercial vehicles. Most traffic accidents are attributed to driver error. Commercial vehicles are no different, but faulty equipment, inoperative brakes, broken steering components, and unsecured loads falling from trailers do account for multiple injuries and death.

Yerington, Nevada is a small community about eighty-five driving miles southeast of Reno. Both the east fork and the west fork of the Walker River join there, and most of the beautiful valley is farming and ranching. Late one afternoon in early summer, a young pregnant woman went into labor. Many residents of small Nevada towns choose to have their children in Reno rather than their small community hospitals, so her husband loaded her in their car, and they headed off to Reno.

Excited about having their first child and exceeding the speed limit just a little, they proceeded north on US Alternate 95 for about six miles when a farm truck, attempting to cross the highway from one field to another, slammed into them, killing the young woman and her unborn baby instantly and seriously injuring the young man.

All evidence at the scene, including tire marks, point of impact, contact damage to both vehicles, and fluid trails put the young couple's vehicle in the travel lane exactly where it belonged and the truck failing to yield to through traffic. The truck driver stated that he saw the car coming as he was trying to cross the highway from one field to another. He applied the brakes to avoid the car, but the brakes didn't work.

A safety inspection was performed on each of the vehicles, and while no problems were found with the car, it was apparent that the truck's brakes were inoperative at the time of the crash. Located within the engine compartment was the master cylinder for the brake system.

The master cylinder which holds the brake fluid necessary for the brakes to work was missing its cap, completely empty of fluid, and had a dirty rag stuffed into it. The poor condition of the master cylinder and the presence of spilled brake fluid throughout the engine compartment was proof that the owner, employees, or both neglected the problem.

The driver of the truck was charged with NRS 200.070 Involuntary Manslaughter, but the district attorney chose not to proceed with the case. When the charges were dismissed, I asked the attorney why the case did not go forward, and I was told that there would most likely be a civil lawsuit where a large sum of money could be awarded to the husband for the death of his wife and child.

Perhaps the farmer was too big of a shot in a small county for the district attorney to go after, or maybe the two of them golfed together every Tuesday, but I sure as hell hope that young man hired a good attorney and took the farmer to the cleaners.

Another day, I arrived at a fatal accident where a driveline came apart on a commercial vehicle. A portion of it called a U-joint bounced off the highway and through the front windshield of a car traveling in the opposite direction. The driver of the car was killed instantly while his wife, who was seated beside him, received minor injuries in the crash that followed.

Most often when commercial vehicle safety inspections are conducted and equipment deficiencies and violations are noted, the drivers are allowed to continue and have them corrected as soon as practical. But if the violations detected are of a serious nature, the vehicle is immediately put out of service and must be either towed to a repair shop or corrected on-site before being allowed to continue.

One of the main check sites where we conducted inspections was on I-80 eastbound at Garson Road, just west of Reno. Most of the commercial vehicles we encountered there had just entered Nevada after driving down the east slope of the Sierra Nevada Mountains from

Donner Pass to the Truckee Meadows. It is a steep, forty-mile, 2,600-foot descent, and I could not count the number of commercial trucks and passenger buses we put out of service at the bottom for bad brakes.

Many of the buses were filled with passengers on their way to gamble at Nevada casinos. These people had just come down one of the largest mountain ranges in America on a bus with bad brakes, and they were delayed an hour or so until a spare bus could arrive, go through an inspection, and whisk them away. Anger is too nice of a word to describe how these people felt about the bus company they had paid to deliver them to their destination.

Commercial vehicle safety is a very important job. I learned a wealth of information, it was great for my career, and I enjoyed doing it—who knew? Well, in retrospect I guess Colonel Bill Yukish and Captain Hood, two men who I admired and respected, knew because it wasn't too long before I was a lieutenant.

A Horrible End to a Wonderful Career

Written by Former Nevada State Trooper Michael Sigman

It was the afternoon of September 8, 1993. I had gotten off work early and was spending the rest of the day at home with my kids. My sister had sent my kids a package, and as I sat there watching my kids playing with their new toys, the telephone rang. It was Kathy McDonald, one of our dispatchers at the Reno office.

From a prepared script, she read, "Trooper Sigman, I want to inform you that Trooper Ken Gager has been transported to Washoe Medical Center by CareFlight after a package exploded at his house in Minden, Nevada. Nevada Highway Patrol Command advises all personnel not to open any packages that they receive if they don't recognize the return address. Also, report any suspicious activity to local law enforcement."

That phone call shook me to my core. I watched my kids playing with their new toys and the empty box they'd arrived in as I sat there trying to process what I'd just been told.

"Holy cow," I thought. "It could have been any of us!"

Four troopers lived in our subdivision, which our shift supervisor, Sergeant Jim Warne, dubbed "Trooper Heights." All Nevada troopers had marked patrol vehicles assigned to them that they took home every night, so it was obvious to all where we lived. I always knew and accepted that we were targets, but to send a letter bomb to our homes was another level.

Before heading to bed that night, I got a call from work that I was to go to Trooper Gager's house once I called on-duty. Early that next morning, I arrived at Ken's house and relieved Trooper Tom Rolfe, who had been there all night. Trooper Rolfe told me that NDI (Nevada Division of Investigation), Douglas County Sheriff's Office investigators, a Douglas County Fire/Bomb Investigator, FBI agents, and United Sates Postal Service inspectors were in the house gathering evidence and doing their absolute best to find out who committed this horrific crime.

Trooper Rolfe wondered if the bomber could have been a person that Ken had arrested two years prior who had left him with an uneasy feeling. Ken had stopped a vehicle that had a temporary license plate displayed in the front windshield. The paper permit on the windshield was faded and so old that it had fallen apart when Ken asked the driver to remove it from the windshield. Ken had decided to issue the driver a citation which the man signed, but when Ken gave the driver his copy, he crumpled it up and threw it on the floor. Ken, who was an outstanding state trooper, realized that the driver was most likely not going to take care of the ticket or appear in court, so he decided to place the driver under arrest, which the law allowed for.

Ken requested the driver exit his vehicle, told him he was under arrest, and to turn around and put his hands behind his back. The man refused Ken's command and just stood there, glaring at him with balled-up fists. Ken got on his radio and requested backup. After a few minutes, the driver told Ken that he didn't want his small daughter, who was the only passenger in the vehicle, to see him get arrested. Ken discreetly took the driver into custody with no further problems. He called for someone to pick up the daughter and requested a tow truck for the vehicle. As Ken booked the man into the county jail, his uneasy feelings intensified. The driver continually glared at him. Trooper Ken Gager was not easily intimidated by anyone, but this guy got to him.

Anytime a person is arrested and removed from their vehicle, an impound form is required, listing the items in the vehicle for safekeeping. While conducting the vehicle inventory, Ken found papers with detailed maps and information evidently compiled for the purpose of burglarizing a vault company in Reno. Realizing that the documents were prepared for the purpose of committing a felony, Ken turned the papers over to state of Nevada criminal investigators for follow up. Ken's investigative skills and the evidence he located in the car resulted in burglary and insurance fraud convictions in state court.

After relieving Trooper Rolfe, I proceeded through the garage past Ken's marked patrol car, a Ford Mustang. On the garage floor, next to the car, were a pair of tattered, blood-soaked sweatpants that Ken had been wearing when the package exploded. Ken's injuries were severe, and his condition was critical. Ken lost his left hand at the wrist, as well as his left eye, had a hole in his abdomen the size of a basketball, and had incurred various other life-threatening injuries.

It had been Ken's birthday that week, and his wife, Deanna, had picked up the explosive package at their rural mailbox. Thinking it was a birthday gift from his son, she returned home and placed it on the center island of his kitchen. Deanna was next to him when he began opening it. There was no return label on it, and he joked about it being a bomb. Deanna was in the process of cooking dinner and had leaned over to retrieve something from the refrigerator when the bomb detonated. Though injured, Deanna was luckily shielded by the refrigerator door and did not receive the devastating injuries Ken incurred.

As I walked into the house, I saw the investigators working and did my best to stay out of their way. My heart sank as I surveyed the damage inside the kitchen and adjoining rooms. The bomb had destroyed the center island, and there were holes from the blast in the floor, ceiling, and adjoining walls. Windows throughout the house had been broken from the concussion.

Ken was my close friend and co-worker, and I wondered if he would survive. I knew from the extent of his injuries that should he live, he would never work as a state trooper again, a job that he loved.

A year before, Ken had showed me the plans of this house, beaming with delight when he got the approval to go ahead with construction. Ken had a background in construction and did quite a bit of the work himself. This was his and Deanna's dream home and had just recently been completed. Now it was violated and destroyed by someone who didn't like what Ken did for a living.

After a couple of hours, two other troopers who worked our district, Mark Zacha and Amy DelSoldato, came by to see the house and to learn if I had any follow-up information on our friend's condition. I remember standing there with them, wondering if this was a targeted attack against Ken or if other highway patrol personnel were going to receive similar packages at their homes. Most of us had spouses and children, and the thought that someone might be targeting state troopers in the area scared all of us.

While speaking with Mark and Amy, Douglas County Bomb Squad detective Steve Kibbe asked if any of us were going to the hospital. I told him that I was going to go when I got off-duty. Detective Kibbe asked me to give something to Deana, who refused to leave her husband's side. Steve reached into his pocket and handed me a wedding band that had been crushed from the blast. It was found embedded in a wooden cabinet in the kitchen. This was another shock to my system as I wondered how in the hell Ken had survived the blast.

The investigators finished gathering what evidence they needed and locked up the residence before leaving. I left shortly thereafter and drove home. I told my wife what happened and remember breaking down and crying a few times. I was changing out of my uniform when Highway Patrol Lieutenant Mike Henry called and told me that I was temporarily assigned as a liaison between our department and the bombing task force, which had taken over a squad room in the Douglas County Sheriff's Office in Minden. As an eight-year veteran of the Nevada Highway Patrol, I had never been part of an investigation of this magnitude. The team of investigators included members of the State of Nevada Investigative Division, Douglas County Sheriff's Office, the Federal Bureau of Investigation, United States Postal Inspection Service and agents from the Department of Alcohol, Tobacco and Firearms. I had heard stories about how getting the feds involved in state-level cases seldom went well, however, during this event, I have never seen so many different agencies work so well together. They were truly a team intent on solving this crime and arresting the perpetrator of this senseless act.

I reported to the sheriff's office, and as I walked into the squad room, I saw a written timeline on the wall. There were a few names up on the board as possible suspects. One of the bombing suspects listed was the guy Ken had arrested and been concerned about two years earlier, Robert Collins.

Within one day, the investigation centered on Collins as the main suspect. The FBI identified him as a former Green Beret and Vietnam War veteran. As more information was being gathered, we learned that Collins was a career criminal who made his living committing insurance fraud by burglarizing storage units, including his own, and then reporting his property as stolen to collect money from insurance companies. Somehow, we learned, Collins had never been arrested or charged for any of his crimes. Some investigators chasing Collins gave him the nickname "No Touch" because he always wore gloves or would pick items up using the heels of his hand so no fingerprints would be left. Collins had a reputation of intimidating anyone who got in his way. While Trooper Ken Gager may have had a bad feeling about this guy, Ken was not the type to back down from anyone. Two years prior, Collins had met his match in Trooper Ken Gager.

We also learned that a few days prior to the bombing, Collins appeared in court because his case was about to go to trial. During the proceeding, Collins actually threatened the judge and then stated that he wanted to kill Trooper Gager. The judge ordered Collins to go through a mental evaluation at the Northern Nevada Mental Health Institute. At the mental hospital the night after the bombing, the headline story on the television news was the bombing of a Nevada State trooper. According to other patients interviewed at the hospital, when it was reported that Ken had survived the blast, Collins reacted violently and had to be restrained. It appeared to all investigators that Collins had moved from a possible suspect to the probable suspect, but there was still a lot of work to do gathering evidence. FBI agents met with the local United States attorneys to obtain a warrant for all phone calls made by Collins while at the Mental Health Institute.

Attention also focused on Collins' wife. Investigators learned that Jeanne Collins was a nurse working in the San Francisco Bay Area, and authorities in that area immediately put Jeanne Collins under surveillance. The following Sunday, Jeanne Collins drove back to Nevada with her young daughter Ashley. As Mrs. Collins pulled into her driveway, she was greeted by several law enforcement officials. While Collins was being questioned, her daughter Ashley was separated and interviewed by an agent of the Nevada Division of Investigation. The female NDI detective was able to build a rapport with Ashley, and the young girl turned out to be a tremendous witness. When asked, Mrs. Collins told investigators she knew nothing about the bombing. She said her husband never told her anything because she had a big mouth.

Jeanne told investigators that when her husband got out of jail, after being arrested by Ken, he became obsessed with getting even. Collins found out where Ken lived in Carson City and placed Ken and his family under surveillance. Somehow, Collins was able to get all of Ken's vital information. Keep in mind, this was long before the internet made this information readily available. Collins would go through Ken's trash and drive by his residence several times a week. When Ken bought the land on which to build his new house, it was just a couple of miles from Collins who, in his disturbed mind, was convinced that Ken was after him. To the best of my knowledge, Ken had no idea that Collins was doing any of this, nor did he know that Collins lived so close to where his new house had been built.

As the NDI detective interviewed Ashley, she had quite a bit to say about the bombing. Ashley told the agent that she and her father had gone to her dad's friend's house, and that the friend's name was Av. While there, she saw her dad and Av working on a box and carrying it around very carefully. When asked, her dad told her that the box was a present for somebody. Ashley said that there were nuts, bolts, batteries, and wires in the box, and when asked, Ashley drew a picture of it.

The next day, when the NDI detective showed the investigative team and bomb technicians the hand-drawn picture, they said this could very well be the bomb that Ken had opened. One of the ATF agents perked up at the name Av and thought it might be a man they had been keeping an eye on for some time regarding probable firearm and explosive ordinance violations. The focus of the ATF agents was a man named Avrom Finkel.

ATF team members showed the group a video of Finkel blowing up an old washing machine with dynamite in an open field. The bomb techs believed that dynamite was used in Ken's bombing, and this could possibly tie Finkel to the case as well. Further investigation revealed that Collins had an extensive electronics background but knew very little about explosives.

On the first day of the investigation, while digging through the rubble, the bomb techs were able to recover a piece of wood that had an imprint of a Micro Switch manufacturer's plate and serial number. Micro Switches are used to lock and unlock doors. Anyone buying a

Micro Switch must have the purchase documented, the serial number listed, and a name of who purchased it. The serial number on that Micro Switch came back to Robert Collins. The bomb techs said that the Micro Switch was used to detonate the bomb. When the lid on the box opened, there were springs on the hinges designed to pop open and activate the Micro Switch.

ATF agents went to Finkel's house and retrieved a lot of information about the bombing. Finkel admitted that he had kept the bomb at his house while awaiting instructions from Collins. The day that Collins was ordered for a mental evaluation, he called Finkel and told him to mail the package. Being in a mental institution was Collins' alibi that he couldn't possibly have mailed a bomb. Collins didn't have any idea that his daughter, Ashley, would be such an important witness and help put her father away for a very long time. When Ashley was asked why she was being so helpful to investigators, she said, "If my daddy did this, he should go to jail."

Phone records acquired from the mental hospital showed Collins made numerous calls to many different phone numbers, but the calls made to Finkel were consistent with what Finkel told the ATF agents.

It was amazing watching these agents and detectives from so many different agencies (federal, state, and local) work so well together to bring this monster to justice. Collins was a career criminal who'd been able to get away with committing numerous crimes for many years, only to be stopped by Nevada Highway Patrol Trooper Ken Gager for not having license plates on his vehicle.

I was able to see Ken at the hospital on the Sunday after the bombing, but he was in a drug-induced coma to help with his recovery. His head was heavily bandaged, and only his mouth and chin were exposed. It was difficult and surreal to see him like this. I left without saying anything to him because I didn't know if he could hear me.

Weeks later, when the investigation was completed, I returned to my duty station in Carson City and resumed my normal duties. A few weeks after getting back to work, I was at the Carson-Tahoe substation when the phone rang. It was Ken! I told him it was so good to hear from him. He sounded very weak, and it was a struggle for him to breathe, but I knew that he was awake and alert.

I went up to see him in the hospital that afternoon, and he told me that his memory of the incident was spotty. There was a bright flash, intense pain, and he felt air where he knew he shouldn't be feeling air. Deanna, somewhat protected by the refrigerator door when the package exploded, was thrown into the refrigerator from the blast and then saw Ken injured on their kitchen floor. Deanna tried calling 911 on her phone and thought the explosion took the phone out of commission. The phone was still working, but temporary deafness from the blast made it impossible for her to hear. The explosion brought out neighbors who called for an ambulance.

I talked to Ken again a few months later. After numerous surgeries and physical therapy, he was finally able to come home from the hospital. Ken recalled being loaded in the Life Flight helicopter and said that he remembered looking down at a large group of his troopers and other law enforcement personnel. In his mind, he saw a coffin draped with an American flag and a trooper's hat at the head of it. He said he thought it was a memory from Trooper Dan Peterson's funeral. Trooper Peterson had been struck by a drunk driver and died from his injuries a couple of years before. Ken told me that when he realized it was his family standing behind the casket, he wasn't going to allow himself to quit even though he was in excruciating pain. He told himself that, "I'm not going to give that (expletive) Robert Collins the satisfaction of killing me." That statement put a lump in my throat and tears in my eyes.

Sometime later, Ken said to me, "When Deanna brought the

package in the house and told me it was for me, I said, 'Why don't you open it. It's probably a bomb.'"

It's not that it was a premonition—it was Ken's sense of humor. Ken said, "I felt uneasy opening the box since I didn't know who it had come from."

A voice in my head screamed out, "Then why did you open it!?" But I guess this is something you don't think of seriously happening in the sanctuary of your own home.

After the bombing, we were all wondering if the state of Nevada would take care of Ken. The first glimmer of hope that he was going to be taken care of was when the state deemed this to be a work-related injury, which meant all his medical costs were covered and he was placed on worker's compensation. The NHP also made a position at headquarters for Ken to work as a trooper. Some people thought it wasn't right that Ken keep his trooper position, as he was considered legally blind, had lost his left hand, and wasn't physically capable to be on the road. But in my humble opinion, he almost paid the ultimate sacrifice for doing his job—it was the least the state could do for him.

In December 1995, Collins was found guilty, and in April 1996, he was sentenced to seventy-five years in federal prison. Collins was forty-seven when he was sentenced, which means he'll be a very old man when and if he ever gets out. His accomplice, Avrom Finkel, was tried separately and sentenced to eighty-six years for his involvement in the bombing and other unrelated weapons charges.

I got the detail and the pleasure, along with Trooper Margaret Amster, of escorting Collins to his sentencing courtesy of the U.S. Marshals. We were briefed by the deputy marshals that we were to provide escort from the Warm Springs Prison in Carson City to the federal courthouse in Reno. They wanted us to travel at an average speed of eighty miles per hour on the highway to discourage any escape attempt by Collins.

We arrived at the courthouse, and Collins was escorted inside, where quite a few of Ken's fellow troopers, friends, and family were present for the sentencing. Ken was in his dress uniform and spoke to the judge prior to passing sentence.

At one point, Ken told Collins, "If you had any moral fiber, you'd kill yourself." Collins replied with something we couldn't hear, and Ken told Collins, "Shut up, Robert."

Collins replied, "Why don't you shut up for a change."

As the tension in the courtroom leveled out, Ken finished saying his piece to the judge. Then Ken squared off at Collins! We all thought Ken was going to attack him. A few people got in front of Ken and walked him away.

After witnessing the tense event, Trooper Amster and I escorted the marshals and Collins back to Warm Springs Prison. It felt good escorting Collins back into the prison where he belonged and will reside for many, many years.

In May 1994, Trooper Ken Gager was invited to be a guest speaker at the annual National Law Enforcement Officer's Memorial Service in Washington D.C. This event is where every law enforcement officer who lost their life in the line of duty the preceding year has their name added to the beautiful granite walls. Ken addressed thousands of officers from all over America and was able convey to them the importance of fighting to stay alive.

After thirteen years of being an NHP trooper, I decided it was time to move on, so I took a job with the Cobb County Police Department outside Atlanta, Georgia. I saw Ken before I left, and we said our goodbyes. I have worked over twenty years with the Cobb County Police Department and was assigned to our training academy for nine of those years. I told many recruit classes this story, not only to honor a brave and good man, but to let the recruits know that no matter how bad you're hurt, you don't ever give up!

Excuses, Excuses

The automobile—what a marvelous invention. Finally, after several hundreds of thousands of years afoot, humans invented and developed one of the most remarkable forms of transportation available. At long last, mankind can relax and at the same time be transported great distances in relatively short periods of time. The ease, the comfort, the leisure, the speed limit . . . Hey, wait a minute! Nobody said anything about a speed limit! Although mankind has long known that along with any freedom comes responsibility, they can forget in a hurry if they are the one who is caught.

The first speeding ticket issued in the United States went to Mr. Harry Meyers of Dayton, Ohio who was traveling at the breakneck speed of 12 miles per hour. Without a doubt, the first issuance of a speeding citation was accompanied by the first excuse for speeding. Having written thousands of speeding citations and hearing close to an equal number of reasons why, I have developed six basic categories for speeding. Though I have no idea what excuse Mr. Harry Meyers used that fateful day in history, I am quite certain that it would have fit into one of the following six:

The "I Didn't Knows":

By far the most common excuse, the "I Didn't Knows" lack creativity and imagination, however, their ability to act sincere while attempting to convince the officer of their ignorance is without question. Common "I Didn't Know" excuses are: "I didn't know I was speeding"; "I didn't know what the speed limit was"; and "I didn't know this road had a speed limit."

The "I Thoughts":

Though not as numerous as the "I Didn't Knows," the "I Thoughts" are a bit more creative. Excuses include, "I thought it was okay to go a little over the speed limit"; "I thought everyone was allowed ten over"; and "I thought the speed limit was sixty-five" (even though they were caught doing ninety).

The "Mechanical Malfunctions":

Not willing to accept any responsibility for the excessive speed of their vehicle, the "Mechanical Malfunctions" are quite adept at transferring blame to inanimate objects such as oversized tires, broken speedometers, and stuck gas pedals. While the first two examples can most certainly be a factor in a person's knowledge of their vehicle's speed, they are commonly used by drivers who were passing the rest of the motoring public like they were standing still. As for stuck gas pedals, I have never seen one and most likely never will.

The "What About the Other Guys":

These drivers attempt to divert the trooper's attention away from themselves and toward others, hoping that the trooper will wish them a good day and speed off to catch someone else. Included in this category are, "I was just keeping up with traffic"; "Everyone was speeding, so why are you picking on me?"; "You only stopped me because I am (fill in the blank with white, black, brown, green, pink, from out of state, etc.); and one of my favorites, "Why don't you go out and catch real criminals?"

The "Honesties":

Far more plentiful than one would think, the "Honesties" have a limitless number of reasons for speeding, many hoping that by fessing up they might just receive a warning. Most common is, "I am late for (again fill in the blank with work, school, a funeral, picking up my children, a job interview, etc.); and medical emergencies (more often perceived than actual).

The "Off the Walls":

Not fitting into other categories, the "Off the Walls" can be very amusing to the traffic officer. Their excuses can be refreshing, humorous, totally made up, unpredictable, and generally keep the job of stopping speeding motorists interesting. Some of my favorites were, "This is the ugliest state I have ever driven across, and I can't wait to get out"; "Me and my three friends are headed to the brothel in Winnemucca and our wives are chasing us"; and "I owe gangsters money and I am trying to get away."

With freedom comes responsibility, which means following rules and laws for the common good and safety of society. Traveling above the designated speed limit increases your chances of being involved in an accident, and the faster you are traveling when an accident occurs, the more likely you are to be seriously injured or killed. Whether the form of transportation be automobiles like today or personalized flying machines or spaceships in the future, there will most likely be speed requirements of some kind, and I am confident these categories of excuses will still apply.

Hey, Sawge, Wi'll Git Ya Cawd

While working as a sergeant in the Reno office, I was put in charge of the Region II Honor Guard. I oversaw a group of sharp-looking troopers who practiced marching and flag folding and represented our department at graduations, funerals, and other events. One year I had the opportunity to take the members of the honor guard and their spouses to Washington D.C. to attend National Police Week at the National Police Officers Memorial celebration. It is a wonderful and humbling trip that I encourage all law enforcement officers in America to make at least once during their careers.

After the police event concluded, my wife Janelle and I took the train from Washington D.C. to Boston, stopping and visiting Philadelphia and New York for three days on the way. Our destination was the original Salem Village, Massachusetts, now called Danvers, where my eighth direct great-grandmother was hung as a witch in 1692. Her name was Rebecca Nurse, and there is a monument dedicated to her on the old Nurse family homestead.

After touring the Danvers area, we decided to head over to the coast and stopped in the town of Gloucester where we toured around and did a little shopping at local stores. In the early evening, we left Gloucester and arrived in the beautiful small town of Rockport. We found a souvenir in a small shop, and when I went to pay for it, I could not find my credit card. I quickly realized that I had left it at the store we had visited earlier in the day in Gloucester. We called the store, but it was after five o'clock and the store had already closed, so the credit card would have to wait until tomorrow. Or would it?

Focused on eating a nice, fresh lobster dinner, which is difficult to obtain in the Nevada desert, we happened to see two Rockport police officers walking their beat and engaged them in conversation. It is no secret that if you want the best meal in any town, ask a law enforcement officer. I told them I was a sergeant with the Nevada Highway Patrol, and we were looking for the best lobster dinner in Rockport. I mentioned that I had accidentally left my credit card at a shop in Gloucester, and we would be paying cash for dinner, so I inquired as to how much two lobster dinners should cost.

These officers were two of the nicest young men you could wish to meet. They asked me if I knew the name of the shop in Gloucester where I had left my credit card, so I looked at my receipt and provided them with the name of the store.

In the thickest Massachusetts accent possible, one of the officers said, "Hey, Sawge. I know the folks who own that stoe."

The officer placed a call to the owners who advised him that I had indeed left my card at their store and that they had it with them at their house in the nearby town of Peabody (pronounced peabiddy).

"Hey, Sawge, wi'll git ya cawd. It will take about fawty-five minutes."

"Wow, guys. That is above and beyond the call of duty. Are you sure you can pull that off?"

"No problem, Sawge. You want that lawbsta dinna while you wait?"

"That would be great," I said.

The two young officers led us into a nice little restaurant right on the dock. It was a cute little place with a dozen picnic tables covered with red and white checkered tablecloths.

The young officer looked at the lady proprietor and said, "Hey, Dawthy. The sawge and his wife want lawbsta for dinna. Take good ceh of em!"

So, while these two fine young men made a forty-mile round trip to retrieve our credit card, Janelle and I had the biggest, freshest, tastiest, lowest-priced lawbsta dinna we had ever had.

The Barrel Went Boom

My older brother by seven years, Bruce Raabe, spent thirteen months hiking through the jungles of Vietnam carrying a rifle for the United States Marine Corps. I graduated from high school right at the tail end of the Vietnam War in 1975, when the military was downsizing like crazy, so I never served. However, if you consider that fewer than fifteen percent of U.S. military enlisted personnel ever see combat or are assigned a combat role, a career as a state trooper, toting a gun to work, risking getting shot, dodging traffic daily, and occasionally wrestling with drunks miles from town with no backup should qualify for something.

Not being in the military, I had no exposure to explosives. Other than setting off a few firecrackers, cherry bombs, and M-80s as a kid, the only time I ever saw anything more powerful was when I was cutting timber in Oregon as a young man. My cutting partner and I felled five big trees, and rather than fall to the ground, all ended up leaning into the top of a big noble fir. There was no way to get under the big mess and cut the noble fir without risking death, so my boss, Jerry Mack, wrapped a few sticks of dynamite around the base of the tree and set it off. It was not as big an explosion as I expected, and all it did was blow off the bark. I was sent off to fall timber in another section and I don't recall how Jerry finally took that tree down. The important thing was that I was nowhere close to the mess when it all tumbled to the ground.

My next and only experience with explosives came fifteen years later as a sergeant in Reno. The Nevada deserts and mountains are home to more old mines than one can imagine. It is hard to go out anywhere and not see holes and piles of tailings where miners scratched out a living in days past. As for old miners, there are few of them left.

One day in 1993, an old miner died in the Virginia Foothills south of Reno. He had spent his life mining for gold and silver in the area, and while going through his outdoor shed, his family came upon a very rusty fifty-five-gallon barrel filled with old dynamite and sweating nitroglycerin.

The Sheriff Bomb Squad was called, and they surveyed the situation. Their plan was to use a front-end loader to place the barrel gently and carefully into the back of a ten-yard dump truck, surround it with numerous sandbags, and move it to a gravel pit thirty miles north of Reno near Pyramid Lake.

The Nevada Highway Patrol was called to shut down all highway traffic and escort the load as it made its way across Reno, Sparks, and Spanish Springs. I led the lengthy convoy over thirty miles to the gravel pit, and luckily we all arrived in one piece. I then positioned my patrol car on State Route 445 (Pyramid Highway) about one mile north of the gravel pit where I would stop all southbound traffic prior to the barrel being set off. Shortly thereafter, I was joined by a large firetruck and several firemen.

It took about an hour to unload the barrel and get it ready to blow. As soon as they finally gave me the word that they were ready, I blocked one lane with my patrol car, and the firetruck blocked the other. I remember looking at the gravel pit across the one-mile stretch of desert and told the fireman that we would probably be lucky to hear the darn thing this far away. Was that an understatement.

When the bomb squad lit the barrel off, there was no sound, but I could see the shock wave moving in all directions across the desert. Sound travels through the air at approximately 1,100 feet per second, so at one mile away it would take about five seconds for the sound to get to us. The shock wave reached us a fraction of a second before the sound and rocked both my patrol car and a forty-thousand-pound fire truck, followed a fraction of a second later by the sound. I am here to tell you the blast of the rusty barrel filled with old dynamite and sweating nitroglycerin did not disappoint. Thankfully, it never exploded and took out the whole neighborhood while stored in the old miner's cabin.

Is There Another Ambulance?

We always wondered who had a hand in designing the interstate system that crisscrossed right through the center of both Reno and Sparks. Did the original highway engineers, now retired, sit on their decks high in the surrounding mountains drinking beer and laughing as vehicles crashed at the same time in the same places every day?

Perhaps it was good old Nevada politics that caused the mess. Everyone knew that state laws were crafted in Jack's Bar or the Old Globe Bar in our state capital of Carson City. The actual legislature building was just a place to vote and house staff. I can close my eyes and hear the law-making conversations that took place in those bars decades ago.

"Senator So and So, I own a casino and by God that freeway is going to have an off-ramp right to my front door. Oh, and I need an easily accessible freeway on-ramp in the same place."

Or "Assemblyman What's Your Name, I own a big casino in Sparks, and I have a great idea. Why don't you build that narrow six-lane freeway right over the top of my casino? Those big concrete freeway supports will make wonderful backdrops for the massive fish tanks in our bar! Don't worry about thirty years from now when those six lanes need to be expanded to ten or twelve. The future will take care of itself."

So, what happens when freeway on-ramps and off-ramps share the same quarter of a mile and a whole mess of cars are entering, merging, changing lanes, and exiting at the same time? Reno Highway Patrol sergeants and their merry band of swing-shift troopers get to handle car wrecks at the same times and the same places every workday for the next thirty years. It was the problem area on I-80 in Sparks, where the freeway went over and through the casino with the lovely fish tanks, that I had the one and only negative run-in with a fellow first responder.

A two-car injury accident had already reduced the travel lanes from three down to one, backing up traffic for miles. In addition to a single lane, the westbound off-ramp at the site of the accident was still open and very much needed. In the gore area, between the travel lanes and the off-ramp, I was tending to an injured man who was lying on the ground.

The local ambulance service was called REMSA, and the paramedics who worked there were very skilled, dedicated, and in my opinion ridiculously underpaid for the difficult, stressful job they perform daily.

I watched as the REMSA driver skillfully worked the big ambulance through and around the backed-up traffic and was quite impressed until he parked it directly in the middle of the off-ramp, blocking the entire exit.

As the paramedic got out, I met him at the driver's door and politely said, "Hello, I am Sergeant Raabe. Could I get you to move your ambulance up about twenty feet and off to the side so I can keep this off-ramp open?"

The young man looked at me and said, "No, my patient is right here next to the road!"

"Yes," I said nicely. "I understand that, and we will be happy to help you move him with the gurney or carry him, but I need to keep this lane open, so could you please move your ambulance up about twenty feet and out of the road!"

The young man again said, "No, I don't think so. My patient is right here, and this is where I am going to park."

Having had enough of this kid but still using a calm, polite voice, I asked him, "Are you the only ambulance working in the Reno area tonight?"

The young man replied, "No, there is another one out and about."

"Well," I said, "you might want to get him on the radio and have him start heading this way."

"Why should I call him? I don't need any help."

"Because if you don't climb back in that ambulance and move it out of the way like I have politely asked of you twice now, your ass is going to be in the Washoe County Jail in as much time as it takes me to slap handcuffs on you and have you carted up there. Now, are you getting a grasp of the situation here?"

I guess he got the drift because he immediately climbed back aboard his ambulance and moved it up about twenty feet and off to the side.

The next day, this young man's supervisor called me at the Reno NHP office, asked why I had threatened to arrest his employee, and wondered why we all couldn't just get along? I explained that I had politely asked his driver twice to move his ambulance, and twice he'd refused. I further advised him that the highway patrol trooper is the one that is in charge and responsible for the entire accident scene, not the fireman, not the ambulance guy, but the state trooper. His driver didn't seem to understand that concept, so I strongly suggested that he explain that to all his employees to avoid any future problems.

Hiring the Best

Early in 1994, I transferred from swing-shift sergeant in Reno to personnel sergeant at headquarters in Carson City. I was living in Carson City and took this position so I could see my wife and children more than two days a week. I could barely spell personnel, and now I was expected to perform a critically important mission. Nothing in the highway patrol is more important than selecting the human beings who will spend the rest of their working lives serving, protecting, and interacting with the residents and visitors of our great state.

When I first started at my new position, we had several troopers facing disciplinary action for numerous crimes, such as soliciting sex on traffic stops and selling drugs out of a patrol car while on duty. Short of being an ex-felon, there were few existing rules or guidelines as to who got hired or who did not. Several lawsuits had been filed against our department for these and other infractions by our personnel.

Two other investigations were ongoing at the same time. One trooper had accidentally shot a commercial vehicle driver at a commercial check site, claiming the suspect made an aggressive movement while in the process of being arrested. There were several other troopers present at the time, and none of them had witnessed anything that could have been mistaken for a furtive movement. The shot that struck the truck driver in the foot bounced off the pavement before hitting the man, so if it was intentional, as the trooper claimed, it was one hell of a bad shot from less than ten feet away.

Another trooper was being investigated by Internal Affairs for a reason I was not privy to, but it turned out that when he was hired by our department, no one looked into his reason for leaving his prior state trooper position. If there's one thing anyone in the position to hire law enforcement officers should know, it's the saying, "Beware the ex-cop looking for a job."

When we started looking into these two troopers' past employment records, we found both had been let go from their previous law enforcement agencies. One had been let go in his probationary period for cowardice. The other had been fired by another state highway patrol for conduct unbecoming of an officer. We were told by that particular state that had we just asked, they would have been happy to share the negative information with us, but to their amazement, no one asked.

Robert Bradshaw, an experienced law enforcement administrator, was our interim chief at the time, and he called me into his office. Chief Bradshaw tasked me with the job of coming up with a way to hire better employees. Faced with this task, I did some research and found a school in California that taught a course called "Police Officer Pre-employment Background Investigation." The course was based on measuring a police officer candidate in fifteen critical areas, and it outlined a set of hiring practices, documentation, standards, techniques, and legal requirements set forth by California POST (Police Officer Standards and Training).

Prior to 1994, Santa Rosa Community College couldn't fill the openings in this seemingly important course; now they couldn't put enough classes on to meet the needs of agencies requesting the training. Negative hiring, retention, and training were the top three reasons for lawsuits against law enforcement agencies nationwide. Recent court decisions held police agencies liable for failing to look into the background of prospective employees. Not so much if they failed to find a past problem, but more so if they failed to look and the negative information was readily available.

I attended the two-week BGI course in Santa Rosa, California. When I returned, Chief Bradshaw asked me if I knew how to hire better troopers. I told him I did. All I needed was a couple of weeks to rewrite the program to comply with Nevada laws and to meet the needs of our department. In addition to that, I needed several troopers statewide to train as background investigators. Chief Bradshaw allowed me to hastily recruit and train seventeen troopers statewide. These people were the first NHP background investigators and were assigned to conduct investigations on a part-time basis.

Within one year's time, the BGI program was instituted department-wide. I then made the program available to other agencies and taught this program to almost every city and county law enforcement agency in Nevada, with the exception of the Washoe County Sheriff's Office and Las Vegas Metro. Both of these agencies, good or bad, already had their own hiring programs in place.

One particular applicant, who did not pass our NHP background, was later hired as a Las Vegas Metro police officer and was subsequently arrested and convicted of indiscriminately shooting and murdering a gang member. On December 27, 1996, the off-duty officer celebrated his thirty-first birthday with family and friends at a local Las Vegas bar. Afterward, he and another off-duty officer drove to a known gang neighborhood, two blocks from the Las Vegas Strip, where he called to a group of known gang members to approach his vehicle. When they did, the officer, while laughing, fired six rounds into the group, hitting one of them directly in the heart. After the officer was arrested, Metro investigators couldn't call quick enough to find out what in his background kept our department from hiring him. The rogue officer was sentenced to life in prison.

The background investigation program we instituted was very thorough, time-consuming, and complex. After an applicant passed a written exam and physical agility test, they were given a thick personal history statement to complete in their own handwriting. This multi-page form required answers to just about any question you could think of that would describe the applicant's life up to that point, such as personal info, school grades, documents and diplomas, teachers' names, complete work history (leaving no time unaccounted for), detailed reasons for leaving prior employment, bosses and co-workers' names (and how to contact them), family members, neighbors, church leaders and friends (and how to contact them), credit histories, bills owed, medical records, driving records, military records, etc.

Each returned applicant file was reviewed for completeness and any obvious reasons to disqualify the applicant at this stage of the hiring process. Those applicants' files that passed the review were assigned and forwarded to a background investigator who had received training on how to interview, verify information and documents, and how to systematically measure each applicant by a set of critical job dimensions required to be a successful, professional law enforcement officer. These job dimensions included integrity, moral/ethical behavior, substance abuse, risk-taking behavior, anger control, confronting and overcoming problems, stress tolerance, conscientiousness, interpersonal relations, communication, decision making and judgment, and the ability to learn.

The best predictor of a person's future is their past. There are very few people in this world who do not have skeletons in their closet or who are perfect in every category. The most important aspect was that the applicant be truthful about their past. It was then up to the chief of the agency to select those applicants who best met our standards.

After being offered a state trooper position, the applicants completed a psychological exam and an interview with a professional psychologist. That was followed by a polygraph examination designed to verify the truthfulness of their answers in the background investigation and to clear up any unanswered questions.

The reason I have gone into such detail about the Nevada Highway Patrol background program, and how it started, is to impress upon those who read this how important it is to hire the best-quality applicants possible. That being said, even a very thorough hiring process can fail to identify an individual's ability to perform the job of a law enforcement officer. Six months in an academy environment and three months of being on the street working under the close supervision of a training officer usually weeded out those who didn't fit.

Those who become law enforcement officers understand that it is a challenging profession. When jobs are plentiful, finding men and women willing to take on the demanding job are few and far between. With the recent nationwide lack of respect for officers, and the acts of violence directed at many of them, people are reluctant to choose our profession. This has resulted in fewer applicants throughout America. In other words, police agencies across our nation are competing for the same applicants leaving those agencies, with low pay and poorer benefits, scraping the bottom of the barrel.

Many people haven't a clue what goes into the selection, training, and hiring of America's law enforcement officers. It's been a long time since the mayor, sheriff, or police chief pinned on a badge and gave a loaded gun to just anyone and then turned them loose on the general public. Things have changed drastically and for the better. Today, the overwhelming majority of American law enforcement officers are painstakingly selected and well-trained. They are among the best in the world and do an exceptional job. But always remember that they are selected from the human race, and once in a while a bad one slips by!

Rubber Meets the Road, or Not

Law Enforcement is a serious, stressful, and often unappreciated business leaving little room for fun at work, but that doesn't mean there can't be an occasional practical joke. This joke was perpetrated long ago upon a Nevada Highway Patrol major by a well-known sergeant, both of whom were assigned to headquarters in Carson City. If it occurred today, you could bet that someone involved would be offended and file a complaint, but at the time, all involved got a good laugh out of it.

On November 15th, a letter was written to Nevada Highway Patrol Chief James Lambert. The letter read as follows:

> *Dear Chief Lambert,*
>
> *The Rubber Manufacturers Association (RMA) is a trade association representing the major rubber manufacturers in the United States. We are most interested in receiving copies of rules from your agency.*
>
> *Would you please send us a list of rules promulgated by your agency so that we may order them as necessary. Please let me know if there is a charge.*
>
> *Many thanks for your help.*
>
> *Sincerely,*
>
> *Peggy Pollock*
>
> *Assistant to the Director, State Government Relations*
>
> *Rubber Manufacturers Association*

No state police or highway patrol chief would handle a request like this, so in short order the letter found its way to the desk of Major Walter T. Hines. As is always the case, the headquarters command officer immediately passed the letter down to a sergeant, who most likely had more administrative assignments and work than he could possibly do.

The sergeant promptly gathered all laws pertaining to the subject and sent them off to Mrs. Peggy Pollock on November 22nd with the following letter:

> *Mrs. Peggy Pollock,*
> *Our rubber rules (laws) are covered by NRS (Nevada Revised Statutes) 545.540 through NRS 545.670. Enclosed, please find a copy of these rules.*
> *If we can be of further assistance, please feel free to contact us.*
> *Sincerely,*
> *Major Walter T. Hines*

NRS 545.540 through NRS 545.670 includes all Nevada laws relating to the sale, use, identification, product standards, distribution, thickness, ointments, and approved lubricants of prophylactics.

On December 26th, a very surprised and somewhat upset Major Walter T. Hines received the following letter from Mrs. Peggy Pollock, Rubber Manufacturers Association, 1901 Pennsylvania Avenue, Washington D.C.

> *Major Walter T. Hines*
> *Nevada Highway Patrol Headquarters*
> *Carson City, Nevada*
>
> *Dear Major Hines,*

We on the staff of the Rubber Manufacturers Association enjoyed reading the regulations concerning prophylactics, however, we can't quite understand why they would be promulgated by the Department of Motor Vehicles and Public Safety (unless it would be somehow connected with "moving violations!").

In all seriousness. The RMA represents the major tire manufacturers in the country such as Goodyear, Goodrich, Uniroyal, etc. As their representatives, we are primarily interested in tire-related rules and regulations.

The Nevada Department of Motor Vehicles sent me a copy of rules and regulations concerning pneumatic tires on December 4. If you have any further regulations which may be of interest, i.e., minimum tread depth requirements, motor vehicle inspection regulations, etc., would you please send them to me?

Thanks for your help.

Sincerely,

Peggy Pollock

RMA

Assistant to the Director

State Government Relations

Shortly after Major Hines opened and read this letter, he walked into Sergeant Thomas Wayne Hammill's office and threw it onto his desk asking, "You, @$$___! Do you know anything about this letter?"

Playing dumb, Sergeant Tom Hammill said, "Well, let me see it" and began reading.

As Tom read through the letter, he slowly and deliberately uttered phrases like, "Hmm, uh huh, whoa, oops, and who knew? It appears from this letter that Mrs. Pollock was inquiring about laws pertaining to tires. Her letter stated implicitly that she wanted rubber rules. (Nevada is the only state in America where prostitution is legal and regulated.) How was I to know she meant tires? And by the way, you're a major, and I am only a sergeant. I don't think you are allowed to call me names!"

This famous event went down in Nevada Highway Patrol history as one of the best jokes ever played and was talked and laughed about for years at many gatherings and Christmas parties. If you think this was the last of Sergeant Tom Hammill's practical jokes, you would be mistaken.

Tom and I worked together in headquarters for a short time and for two years as swing-shift sergeants in Reno. Tom was a lot of fun to work with and made an already enjoyable job that much better.

Paper Clip Counter

The fun part about being a law enforcement officer is interacting with the general public. The difficult part of law enforcement is the intra-departmental politics, favoritism, personalities, and general improprieties, known more commonly as bullshit. All good officers complain about work issues, and every administration seems eager to provide them with something to complain about.

Sometimes the reasons for complaints were on a department or division-wide scale. For example, one time someone way above the trooper level decided to save money and instead of paying per-diem for meals at our academy, instituted a new rule that all highway patrol cadets attending our live-in academy, and all troopers who taught or attended classes there, would eat their meals at the medium-security state prison. So, for well over a year, until our association filed a complaint with OSHA, we were expected to eat our meals at the charming medium-security prison dining room, prepared and served by inmates, many of whom we had arrested. As far as I knew, not one trooper, including me, ate one meal at that facility, but our cadets who lived in the academy dorms had no other options.

Another example was when one of our colonels promoted troopers who worked for him in his personal concrete business on their days off. The colonel found a way to promote some of these "special" individuals by using an obscure personnel rule called "under-filling." Instead of filling open supervisory positions with people from the current promotional list, the colonel would fill them with troopers from the cement crew. The rest of us were required to study, take written and oral exams, and compete for the leftover openings. We thought the colonel was sprinkling fairy dust on these people, but it turned out it was cement powder.

Often, reasons for complaints were on a more personal level. Region commanders were captains or majors and were somewhat autonomous. They were normally allowed to run their regions as they saw fit. If the commander didn't particularly care for you or you for them, your existence working for them could be difficult. I experienced this first-hand when I promoted to lieutenant.

I was living and working in Carson City and was high on the promotional list when an open lieutenant's position was first offered. The position was in the Elko Region on the other side of the state. Had it just been my wife Janelle and me, we would have packed our stuff and left that night, but two of our children were still at home. At the time, our son, Mike, was working toward an Air Force Academy appointment, and moving would have made a difficult process impossible. The rule at the time was that if you accepted a position, you had to remain in it for at least one year, so I turned the position down. It was offered to another sergeant who worked in my area, and he accepted the position and moved to Elko. No other positions were available at the time.

Four months later, one of four lieutenant positions opened in Region #2. This region covered the entire northwestern portion of Nevada, including Carson City, so no move was required. The colonel called me into his office and offered me the position, and I gladly accepted. Lieutenant Raabe—you must admit those two words sounded good together. The Nevada Highway Patrol Special Order, promoting me to lieutenant and assigning me to the open position in Reno, was sent out statewide. That's when the trouble began.

The captain in charge of the Reno Region was a bona fide member of the cement crew. Immediately upon hearing the news that I was to be the new lieutenant assigned to his region, the captain contacted the colonel and requested that the lieutenant, who had previously been promoted and assigned to Elko four months earlier, be allowed to take that position and that I take the Elko spot. The colonel told the captain that wasn't happening and that I was going to be his new lieutenant.

There were five lieutenant positions available in the Reno Region at the time, four supervising operations in different geographical areas and one over administration. The admin lieutenant supervised the clerical staff in the front office, the dispatch center, courts and warrants, special officers, the radio shop, vehicle mechanics, and any other non-operational duties. I would be happy with anything I was assigned.

The day came, and I reported to my new boss who informed me that I would be taking the administrative lieutenant position. There was a lot to learn in that job. It was day shift with weekends off, so I was very excited at the news. That is, until a few seconds later when my new boss informed me that the dispatch supervisor, the courts and warrants section, the radio shop technician, vehicle mechanics, the front office staff, and the administrative sergeant who oversaw them all would be reporting directly to him. He told me that my new office was next door to his and that I was dismissed.

My new boss wanted the other lieutenant and didn't get him, so he made me "The King of Nothing," just like the song. So there I sat, day after day in my office, at my desk with nothing to do but answer the phones. And answer the phones I did! Every time the business phone or the department-wide highway patrol hotline phone which connected directly with every NHP office in the state rang, I answered it with, "Nevada Highway Patrol, Lieutenant Raabe, paper clip counter. Send me your paper clips or staples, and I will supply you with an accurate count."

Calls from within the department always generated questions from my peers about counting paper clips. Calls from the public usually resulted in an awkward pause before asking how I could help them.

For over one month, numerous times a day, I answered the phone exactly as I described. It wasn't long before every highway patrol office in the state knew I had been relegated to the position of paper clip counter.

One day, I had to return to my previous position at headquarters personnel office to meet with the sergeant who had taken over my job. A few minutes later, the colonel walked by, saw me sitting in my old office, and told me that he wanted to see me in his office in ten minutes.

As I sat before the colonel who I had worked with years before when he was a lieutenant, he looked at me with half a grin and said, "Lieutenant Raabe, I understand from several different sources that you count paper clips and staples these days. What is that about?"

When I explained the entire situation to the colonel, his half-grin disappeared, and I think I might have actually seen some smoke coming out of his ears.

The colonel simply said, "Thank you for the information, lieutenant. That will be all!"

I arrived at my office the next morning and was seated at my desk when the captain poked his head in my door and politely said, "I need to see you in my office."

That morning, I was miraculously reassigned as the Reno Urban District Commander, supervising all operations sergeants and troopers assigned to the Reno, North Lake Tahoe District. The only thing the captain had to say was, "I had you in the Administrative Lieutenant position for your own good, and now I think you are ready to take command of a very busy area."

That is exactly the kind of unnecessary strife that makes law enforcement hard sometimes. The criminals on the streets, DUIs, and bad car wrecks were easy compared to the office politics. My short-lived job as the division paper clip and staple counter came to an end, but the captain remained a thorn in my side.

Politics, a Sad Fact of Life

As a young lieutenant, I was working as the Reno Urban Traffic Commander and was quite happy doing so until one afternoon my chief called and informed me that I was being reassigned to the Director's Office in Carson City.

"Director's Office, sir?" I gasped. "I didn't know we had a lieutenant's position in the Director's Office?"

"Well," he said, "it's a one-year assignment, and you will be the first. Finish up in Reno and report a week from Monday."

"Yes, sir. The Director's Office, a week from Monday," I said, still flabbergasted.

The director of the Nevada Department of Public Safety was appointed by the governor to oversee every division under DPS, including the Nevada Highway Patrol, the Division of Investigation, State Fire Marshall Office, Parole and Probation, Peace Officers Standards and Training, Capitol Police, and the Office of Criminal Justice Assistance.

The man that filled this position was Mr. James Weller who had recently retired from the Federal Bureau of Investigation. Mr. Weller culminated his FBI career as the Special Agent in Charge of Las Vegas and prior to that he was an officer in the Marine Corps. I knew little of the man and certainly didn't like a couple of the changes he had made that negatively affected the Nevada Highway Patrol, but I guess I was going to get to know him much better.

I arrived at the Director's Office on Monday morning as scheduled and was shown to my new office, right next door to Deputy Director Ray Sparks. Ray had previously been a major in the Nevada Highway Patrol and the director of the Department of Motor Vehicles. He was one of the most intelligent men I had ever met but was known to analyze everything from every angle before implementation, earning him the nickname, "Paralysis by analysis." I met with Mr. Weller and Mr. Sparks, and they both thanked me for taking the position. I certainly didn't tell them that I had no choice in the matter.

My new job would be conducting audits, research studies, facilitating the adoption of department policies, implementing new directives, attending DPS chief's meetings, and trying not to upset people in positions of higher authority when directed to step on their toes, which can be very awkward and detrimental to one's future career.

My first assignment was to research the labor costs of the Highway Patrol Governor's Security Detail which had just completed its first year of providing full-time security to our governor and his immediate family. The detail was staffed by a full-time lieutenant (rumored to be a good friend of the governor) and several troopers across the state.

Director Weller advised that both he and the chief of the highway patrol were concerned with the amount of money and needed to know the exact amount on wages over the first year. Mr. Weller said he had contacted the governor's chief of staff regarding his concerns and was told to not worry about it.

After obtaining a roster of all personnel who worked the detail, I pulled every bi-weekly timesheet submitted by each of them over the one-year period and went to work. In the highway patrol at the time, we had telegraph, telephone, and tell-a-trooper, so like the leaky FBI of present, there were no secrets.

The very next day, when I arrived at work, Mr. Weller called me in and said that he had received a phone call regarding me researching the timesheets. During the call, it was stated that the lieutenant who oversaw the program was not happy that I was going through the timesheets and further claimed that he and I had never gotten along.

Mr. Weller asked, "Is that true?"

"Well, sir," I replied, "I think our relationship has improved over the years. The last time he hung the phone up on me, he didn't call me a bad name first."

Mr. Weller smiled and advised me to carry on with my assignment.

Several days later, I arrived at some very interesting conclusions. The lieutenant in charge had been the recipient of most of the wages spent during that first year and had been paid for every hour of every day over the one-year period, except for two weeks when he was out of the area on vacation. Pay included normal lieutenant pay for five eight-hour days (forty hours per week), two hours of call-back pay five days a week paid at time and a half, on-call pay at 5% of the remaining fourteen hours of each of the five workdays and forty-eight hours of every scheduled two days off. The lieutenant was at the governor's beck and call, so he did have to respond to work quite often at the governor's request, which was paid overtime.

I completed my detailed report and presented it to both Director Weller and Deputy Director Sparks, who advised me to keep this information to myself. I was then given my next assignment and moved on.

About two weeks later, I walked into my office and found a note to report immediately to Deputy Director Sparks. I walked into his office where he looked at me and said in a disgusted tone, "Lieutenant Raabe, I asked you to keep the details of the governor's security audit to yourself!"

Quite surprised by his statement, I assured him that I had not mentioned the results of the report to anyone.

Director Sparks smiled at me and said, "I'm just messing with you. Get a look at this."

He placed a copy of the front-page of the *Carson City Appeal* newspaper on his desk in front of me. Blazoned across the top was the headline, "Driver Outearns Governor!" According to the story, the highway patrol lieutenant/driver in charge of the security detail earned more in wages that year than Nevada's governor did. Boy did that cause a stink!

Mr. Weller informed me that when he had warned the Governor's Office about the cost of the program and how much the lieutenant had made prior to the word getting out, he was told to mind his own business. When questioned about the situation, the Governor's Office told the media that it was not their problem—it was up to the chief of each division to monitor and control their individual budgets.

When the legislature convened, certain legislators were up in arms about the recent "Driver Outearns Governor" headlines. My chief, who had been concerned over this for months and had brought it up with his boss, who brought it up with the Governor's Office several times, had to go before the entire legislature, beg forgiveness, and assure them that it was all his fault and that it would never happen again. Sadly, my chief became the governor's political scapegoat.

As mentioned earlier, prior to my assignment in the Director's Office, I didn't like some of Mr. Weller's decisions that negatively affected the highway patrol division, but after understanding why Mr. Weller had taken those actions, it made perfect sense. I really enjoyed my one-year assignment working in the Director's Office and greatly admired Mr. Sparks and Mr. Weller, both of whom turned out to be some of the finest men I had the pleasure of working with.

Airplanes on the Highway

O ne bright and sunny mid-morning, I was patrolling I-80 near the tiny town of Golconda. As I drove westbound down Golconda Summit, I noticed a small red plane flying west, just north of the interstate. It appeared to be lining up with State Route 789. SR 789 is a long, straight highway with good visibility that parallels I-80 east from Golconda for several miles before making a turn to the north. Since it looked like the pilot was preparing to land on the highway, I headed in that direction, arriving just in time to watch him set the flaps, followed by a beautiful landing. SR 789 had suddenly become a runway and taxiway as the Cessna 172 continued into town.

I activated the emergency overhead lights and followed the plane until it pulled off the highway and stopped in the small dirt parking lot of a bar called Waterhole #1. Planes are not equipped with rearview mirrors, so the pilot didn't have a clue that I was directly behind him until he stopped and I pulled up alongside. I advised dispatch that I was out with a red Cessna and gave her the N number.

I was a new trooper and I admit that I didn't know any airplane rules, nor could I find anything in the small law library I kept in my patrol car that dealt with planes landing on a highway, but I had to believe that it wasn't ok.

As the pilot climbed out of the plane, I asked for some identification. I didn't know whether to ask for a driver's license or a pilot's license, so I told him any picture ID would work. He handed me a Nevada driver's license. The man was a rancher who owned a place about forty miles away.

"What on earth are you doing landing your plane on a state highway and taxiing into town?" I asked.

"I am picking up a friend to go for a ride," he said.

"Are there any plane rules that allow or restrict you from doing such a thing when it isn't an emergency?" I asked. "And before you answer, you need to know that I will be researching your reply. I know who you are, and I will come after you if you try to bullshit me!"

The pilot told me that he was not allowed to do such a thing and that he knew better. There was so little traffic on the remote highway, and it had such great visibility that he thought he could get away with it. About that time, his friend pulled into the parking lot to get his ride.

I told the pilot, "Climb back in your plane and get it off this highway. If your friend wants a ride, he can meet you at the airport like normal people do. Don't let me catch or hear of you doing this again!"

I drove a half-mile down SR 789 and made sure there was no traffic coming while the small red plane taxied onto the highway and took off in the direction of Winnemucca.

The next occurrence was on US 95 just north of the Winnemucca city limits. I was on patrol, again in the morning, and arrived in the area just in time to see a small plane pull off US 95 and into the parking lot of a farm equipment company. This was another Nevada rancher who needed a part for his tractor and decided it would be much quicker to fly to the parts store and land on the highway rather than go to the airport.

The result was the same. After taking a great big bite out of his rear end, I allowed him to take off. This highway was much busier than the previous one, so I had to stop traffic. The man's name was Tony, and about a year later, he started dating our highway patrol secretary. We became friends, and he was a great guy, swearing he would never try that stunt again.

One summer morning, I was on patrol on I-80, westbound, near the west Winnemucca city limits. The highway in this area makes a big sweeping curve to the right and raises in elevation as it comes out from under an overpass. The visibility is poor toward the west until completing the curve. As I came out of the curve, there was a small tan airplane flying eastbound right over the westbound lanes. It couldn't have been eight feet off the ground, and its two front wheels were headed right for my windshield. For a second or two, I thought I was going to die in a plane crash. I ducked as the plane passed over my patrol car.

I didn't know who this guy was, but I was going to find out, and this one wasn't getting off with a warning. After the plane passed over my patrol car, it immediately gained in elevation. When I pulled off to the side of the road and got out of my patrol car, which didn't take long, it was already several hundred yards away and headed east. I couldn't see the N number on the plane, but it appeared to be an older model covered with fabric instead of metal.

I advised my dispatch center what had occurred and took off immediately for the Winnemucca Airport. The Winnemucca Airport is very small, and if the plane had been there, they would know.

I arrived at the airport and met with the operator. Bingo! The plane had just taken off and was headed to Elko for a scheduled stop. Elko dispatch relayed the information to Trooper Jim McKowan, who drove to the Elko Airport and was present when the little tan fabric plane arrived. He gathered all information on the pilot and the plane. I wrote a report on the incident and forwarded it to the Federal Aviation Administration.

It turned out the pilot was a police officer from southern California who was on vacation with his wife. His wife was traveling eastbound in her car while her husband was flying eastbound in the westbound lanes blowing kisses and waving to her. That explains why he was flying so low. I never heard what happened to him, but I bet you he received a spanking of some kind from the FAA.

Another event took place late one afternoon on US 395 between Carson City and Minden, Nevada. US 395 is a major north/south highway that runs from Mexico to Canada through four western states. The pilot had run out of fuel about two miles south of the Minden Airport. He set his plane down on US 395 northbound in a space between cars and brought his plane to a stop right off the edge of the highway in the dirt. This was the only time I experienced a plane landing on a highway that was in trouble and in dire need of landing.

The embarrassed pilot was in radio contact with the airport and requested that they bring him fuel. After dumping enough fuel into his plane to complete the two-mile trip to the Minden Airport, we shut down all traffic so he could take off safely.

On November 13, 1998, two planes carrying three people collided in mid-air directly over the small town of Yerington, Nevada. Both planes were 1,000 feet in the air about one mile south of the airport when one plane clipped the tail of another as both were coming in for a landing. According to witnesses, it looked as if one plane had tried to avoid the other at the last second but was unsuccessful. One plane carrying a lone pilot crashed into a house, setting it on fire. The other, carrying a local flight instructor and his student, crashed onto a driveway between two homes. All three were killed instantly.

The Yerington Airport is right on the edge of town and is uncontrolled airspace, so it is up to each of the pilots to advise others of their location and intentions. Sadly, there had been a breakdown in communication that day.

As the NHP lieutenant in charge of rural northern Nevada, I was directed by my superiors to respond to Yerington and lend any assistance the Yerington Police Department may need in dealing with the situation. I contacted the area sergeant and several troopers, and all of us arrived shortly thereafter.

Pieces of wreckage were scattered for blocks, and since all three victims were residents of the small town, it was a sad day for the locals. After removing the victims' bodies, several hours were spent locating and protecting debris from the crash until the FAA investigators arrived on scene to begin their investigation.

My last experience to relate is about a crash I missed. In 1983, a few days before Christmas, a very large snowstorm had arrived in the late afternoon and evening, and Winnemucca was getting hit hard. I was working swing shift and had been working several snow-related traffic accidents on I-80 west of town. I have been out on Nevada roadways at night when it was snowing so hard that the only way to find the pavement was to look out the driver's side window for the reflective road markers. This was one of those nights.

I didn't know it at the time, but a medevac plane was trying to land at the Winnemucca Airport to pick up a critical patient and transport him to Reno when radio communication with the plane was lost. The plane had come down two miles short of the airport, right on the side of I-80 and very close to the Rose Creek Interchange. Two people were killed, and one was severely injured. Remarkably, I'd driven right past the crash shortly after it occurred and never saw it.

A small area of the Nevada desert is usually quite easy to search unless one is doing so in the dark during a raging snowstorm. Knowing the plane had gone down west of Winnemucca, it wasn't long before other officers and firemen were out helping to locate it. The crash was found near where I had been working earlier, and it always bugged me that I hadn't noticed it, but that's the way things go sometimes. I learned early in my career that accidents are going to happen, and as a first responder, sometimes you will save some folks and sometimes you won't.

Ratting Out a Friend

In 1992, I was promoted to sergeant and transferred from duty station Winnemucca to duty station Reno. My wife Janelle was able to transfer to a DMV position in Carson City, so that is where we decided to live. The highway between Reno and Carson City at the time was dangerous, and the more patrol cars on it the better, so I was allowed to drive my patrol car the twenty-eight miles to and from work every day.

The house we bought in Carson City had a small, leaky, shallow concrete pond in the front yard. It had green water, a couple of water lilies, and a few fish that barely clung to life. Over the next three years, Janelle had a great time researching and learning about her pond. On a trip to Las Vegas, we visited Nevada Water Gardens and bought a small filter that we added to our pond. In a matter of days, that little filter turned our green water crystal clear. It was the first time we had ever really seen our fish.

Then one day, Janelle informed me that she wanted to start a pond business. We studied, learned as much as we could in a short time, and started Oasis Water Gardens. We worked out of our garage and backyard for three years before opening a store in Reno/Sparks that took off like a rocket. Before long, we had eight full-time employees, four at the store who sold pond supplies, fish, water plants, etc., and four working outside of the store, cleaning, servicing, repairing, and building Koi ponds and water gardens. I was promoted to lieutenant, and every waking moment for the next six years, I was either supervising state troopers and sergeants or I was working on ponds.

One day, I was on patrol on US 50, near the town of Fallon, when suddenly an approaching car pulled out to pass another and was in my lane coming right at my patrol car. To avoid a head-on collision, I hit the brakes and swerved to the side of the highway and into the dirt as the car whizzed by.

"Oh boy," I said. "This driver is not getting away without a citation for this one."

I spun around, and as I was catching up to the vehicle, it stopped on its own and pulled to the side of the highway. I approached the vehicle and immediately recognized the driver as one of my pond customers, Duane. A retired dentist and as nice a guy as you could ever meet, I'd been to his house numerous times to clean and repair his water feature.

"Duane, what was that about?" I asked.

"I don't know," he said. "I just didn't see you, but as soon as I pulled out to pass, I knew I was in trouble!"

"Well, Duane," I said, "I am going to need your driver's license, registration, and proof of insurance."

I returned to my patrol car and wrote my customer and friend a citation for improper overtaking and passing on the left without sufficient clearance.

Duane was not the least bit upset and said he expected a ticket for that move. After the business portion of the stop was completed, we sat and chatted on the side of the highway for several minutes before each of us went our separate ways.

I returned to Duane's house a time or two to work on his water feature over the next six months. No more was said about the ticket until one day when he and his wife came into our store to buy some pond supplies and fish food.

I was ringing up the sale and said, "You know, Duane, I really appreciate your business and the fact that writing you that citation didn't stop you from coming into our store and doing business."

Duane shot me a look right before his wife asked, "What citation?"

Oh, did I feel like a crumb. It wasn't enough that I'd written him a big ticket. No, I had to rat him out to his wife!

With some slipping and sliding and a little double-talk, Duane and I got through that awkward moment at the store as best we could. A few weeks later, I had a chance to apologize to him, and thankfully all he could do was laugh.

Read the Fine Print

Getting older is a blessing. So many people never get the opportunity to grow old, so it doesn't seem right that those of us who do complain about it—but we do. As we age, most of us get slower, less coordinated, and put on a few pounds. But the most annoying aspect for most, including law enforcement officers, is losing their keen eyesight and finally admitting that wearing reading glasses is a necessity.

The Nevada Highway Patrol required troopers to have good eyesight as a condition of employment. To be eligible for employment with our agency at the time, you had to have perfect 20/20 vision or no worse than 20/100 uncorrected vision, corrected to 20/20.

As a young trooper, I was stationed in Winnemucca, Nevada with five other troopers and our sergeant. All of us were in our twenties and thirties except for our sergeant, Mike Curti, who was in his early fifties. For him, presbyopia (the diminishment in the ability to see objects close) had already set in. The remedy for presbyopia is the use of reading glasses. Sergeant Curti would stand before the target at the range with his .357 revolver in hand, reading glasses low on his nose, and his head bobbing like a chicken as his focus continually switched between the weapon's front sight and the target down-range. All of us greatly admired and respected our sergeant, so we were careful not to let him see us smile as he blasted away. It was quite funny to watch the older guys shoot when we were young, but every one of us laughing that day ended up retiring from the highway patrol and resembled head-bobbing chickens at the shooting range in our later years.

Finally admitting to yourself that your close-up eyesight is going is a difficult thing for numerous reasons: vanity, denial, laziness, etc. Most people put off wearing readers far beyond the time they should. This story is about a fellow trooper and dear friend of mine, Jim McKowan, and the one traffic stop that changed his mind about wearing his readers.

Trooper McKowan was stationed in Elko, Nevada for many years. He had come to the realization that he needed reading glasses and had several pairs in his patrol car. However, when he made a traffic stop, he refused to wear his readers on the first approach to the violator's vehicle. After meeting with the driver and obtaining the required documents, Trooper McKowan would return to his patrol car where he would don his glasses and proceed with his business.

One day, he pulled over a passenger vehicle with dad driving, mom in the passenger seat, and their two teenage children in the back. As was common, Trooper McKowan, while looking at the man's driver's license but not able to read anything on it, asked the man if he still lived at the same address.

"Actually, I do not," the man replied. "My wife and I got married years ago, had two children, and with the larger family, we found that the place was just too small for all of us, so we had to move."

Trooper McKowan advised the man that he would get his current address from him in a few minutes and returned to his patrol car. For reasons unknown to Trooper McKowan, everyone in the car began to laugh, which quickly turned into the entire family howling, roaring, and snorting.

Once seated in his car, Trooper McKowan slipped on his readers and, finally able to read the fine print, looked at the man's driver's license. The place the family had moved from, the place that had become too small when the couple had children, the place that just didn't fit anymore, was a post office box.

Trooper McKowan returned to the car with citation in hand, obtained the driver's signature, and concluded his business, but the laughter didn't stop. It was then that he vowed to never leave his glasses in the car again on the first approach. So much for vanity.

Rock Hard Proposal

As remote and desolate as it was, motorists on US 50 rarely saw a state trooper. As you can imagine, that was fine and dandy with them—unless they were having vehicle trouble. Then they wondered where the heck we were.

One summer evening, I was on patrol about ten miles east of Fallon when I noticed a green Chevy Camaro stopped off the south roadway edge with its emergency flashers on. The area on both sides of the highway consisted of alkali and salt flats, the remnants of an ancient dry lakebed. Rocks of numerous sizes had been brought in to build the road base across these mineral flats. I'd grown up in Fallon, and for as long as I could remember, people would collect these rocks and make words and symbols with them in the desert for others to see as they drove by. Names, words, peace symbols, and rock art were common creations, but tonight's message was different.

I approached the Chevy on the driver's side and noticed a young man in the driver's seat and a young woman in the front passenger seat. The young lady was crying, and the young man didn't seem to be at all upset.

"Are you kids alright?" I asked. "Are you broken down?"

"We are fine," said the young man.

"Why then are you stopped on the side of the highway?" I asked. "There is a very small gravel shoulder in this area, and it's not the safest place to stop."

The young man said they were finished and would be on their way.

"Finished with what?" I asked.

The young man directed my attention to a series of dark rocks in the white alkali desert off the side of the highway which read, "Will you marry me?"

I smiled and asked the young lady, "Well, what did you say?"

With tears in her eyes and big smiles on both of their faces, she said, "I told him yes!"

That was my favorite motorist assist of all time.

Snoring at Its Best

When I first began my career, Nevada State troopers were all trained as Emergency Medical Technicians. The medical training was excellent and served me well throughout my career. Most law enforcement officers, and troopers hired a few years after my academy class, were not required to take this special training and were allowed to take a watered-down version called "First Responder Training." The new training only scratched the surface of what we learned as EMTs.

Working as a lieutenant, I was assigned as the Reno Area Rural Commander. The area I supervised covered about 33,000 square miles of Nevada. I lived in Carson City, but my office was in the town of Fallon. Several times a week, I made the sixty-five-mile trip back and forth to Fallon.

One summer afternoon, in 1998, I was driving westbound near Lake Lahontan when dispatch advised me of an injury accident on Alternate US 95, approximately four miles south of Silver Springs. The injured driver was a white male adult who hadn't been wearing a seat belt and was ejected from the car as it overturned. Two Lyon County deputies were at the scene of the rollover and would stand by until I arrived. I was about ten minutes away, so I proceeded to the call.

As I pulled up to the rollover, I observed an older, gray, Dodge, four-door sedan resting on its top, about sixty feet east of the north roadway edge. The vehicle had sustained extensive damage from the rollover.

I was met at the scene by two young Lyon County deputies. I had been working the road close to twenty years, and neither of these two guys could have had much more than twenty weeks of experience. I asked them the condition and the whereabouts of the injured man, and one of the deputies told me that he was lying faceup in the dirt, on the other side of the wrecked car. They had just left him to meet me when they saw me coming down the highway.

"How badly is he injured?" I asked as I was retrieving my medical kit from my trunk.

"Well," said one of the deputies, "it's hard to tell. He's asleep."

"He's asleep?" I asked, incredulously. "What makes you think he's asleep?"

"He's snoring," one of the deputies said.

"A guy rolls his car, gets ejected into the dirt, and then he falls asleep? I don't think so, but let's go see."

We walked into the desert, past the overturned car, and there he was—a white male, in his mid-forties, lying faceup in an awkward position. He had obvious injuries, was bleeding, had a hint of cyanosis (beginning to turn blue), and he was indeed snoring.

"See," said one of the deputies. "I told you he was asleep."

"Yeah, he's snoring, you guys, but it's not because he's asleep. It's because he's unconscious, and his chin is touching his chest. His airway is restricted, and he can't get a decent breath!"

When a person's airway is restricted, it is imperative that it be opened immediately, and several precious minutes had already passed. Opening an airway can be done one of two ways. Either by lifting the chin and tilting the person's head back, or in the case of a person already lying on their back and suspected of having a serious head and neck injury, by keeping the head still and thrusting the jaw forward. Since this man was very likely to have head and neck injuries, it was time to teach these deputies how to perform the jaw thrust maneuver.

I had one of the deputies get on his knees at the man's head and showed him how to use his fingers to gently grasp the man's jaw and lift it forward. Since it was the young deputies' first time seeing this, we performed the jaw thrust together. The man's snoring ceased immediately, and his color began to improve.

Several minutes passed before an ambulance arrived with the professionals needed to take over the man's care. Maybe these very basic medical procedures were taught to these young deputies in their academy, or maybe they were not. But I am positive these two young officers never mistook a closed airway for snoring again.

Who Wants the Ticket?

Turn lanes (also commonly referred to as center turning lanes, two-way left turn lanes, and "suicide lanes" by law enforcement) were developed in the late 1900s and are in use across America today. These lanes are designed to improve the flow of traffic and reduce rear-end collisions by allowing drivers to safely turn left without interfering with through traffic. You will typically see these lanes, marked by solid yellow painted lines, in rural business districts where a high number of vehicles make left turns between intersections. Painted within the center turn lanes are opposing white turn arrows. These confusing arrows are to indicate that traffic traveling in both directions are allowed to use this lane to complete left turns and left turns only.

Drivers intent on making a left turn into a driveway, a parking lot, a business, or a U-turn should signal about three hundred feet before their turn, ensure the lane is clear (since vehicles approaching from the other direction use it as well), slow down, move into the center turn lane, and complete the left turn when traffic allows. Many jurisdictions have laws limiting the distance traveled in the center turn lane before making a left turn.

The problem is that most drivers who use these lanes do so improperly. The most common mistake is driving into the center turn lanes from a private driveway and then merging into traffic. Stopping, parking, or passing another vehicle in the center turn lane is also prohibited. Just so you know if you use the center turn lane improperly, you can receive a citation. If an accident occurs, you will be at fault. Who cares, you ask? Well, to put it bluntly, your average local highway patrolman will.

One afternoon, I was driving westbound on West Williams Avenue in my hometown of Fallon when I noticed a large commercial tractor-trailer with its emergency flashers on stopped in the center turn lane. I pulled in behind the semi and activated my overhead lights. As I climbed out of my patrol car, the truck driver jumped out of his truck and walked back to me.

"Good afternoon," I said. "Are you broken down? Do you need a tow truck?"

"No," he said. "I pulled over here to load up some things to take to Reno."

"What things?" I asked.

"I'm not sure," he stated nervously. "Some guy running a charity called on the CB radio asking if there was a big truck that could take some donated items to a charity in Reno. I volunteered, and he told me to meet him here."

About that time, a small passenger vehicle pulled up directly behind my patrol car and parked. A man got out, and as he walked up to me, I immediately recognized him as J. J. Christy, a popular Reno radio celebrity who did a lot of charity work in the community. I had never met him, but I had seen him in his underwear before. Once a year in the wintertime, he would broadcast his show while standing outside in a snowstorm wearing nothing but a pair of boxers, collecting money for charities. Mr. Christy began to speak, and I motioned for him to stop and wait as I was still in the middle of a conversation with the truck driver.

"Let me get this straight," I said. "Someone asked you to stop and park this truck in the middle of the center turn lane of a highway for the purposes of loading things into your trailer? You must want a ticket today."

"No, sir. I don't want a ticket," the truck driver said. "I was just trying to help!"

Mr. Christy, unwilling to wait any longer, blurted out, "I am J.J. Christy, and this is all my fault. I asked him to stop here and help me out."

I looked at Mr. Christy and asked in a serious voice, "So then, Mr. Christy, you want the ticket for illegal parking today?"

Mr. Christy looked surprised and said, "Well, I asked this man to stop, but I don't really want a ticket."

I immediately turned to the truck driver and asked, "So, you want the ticket?"

The driver stated again, "No, I don't want the ticket."

I looked at both Mr. Christy and the truck driver and asked as seriously as I could, "Do you gentlemen want to discuss among yourselves which one of you is getting a ticket today, because this truck is illegally parked, and someone is getting one!"

They both gave each other a shocked look as I continued. "Mr. Christy, I appreciate all you do for the community, and you're down here in Fallon doing more, so I really don't want to give you a ticket."

"Mr. Truck Driver, I appreciate your willingness to help and volunteer your time and truck to someone you don't even know, so I really don't want to give you a ticket either. Yes, gentlemen, this is quite the dilemma."

I could contain myself no longer as I smiled at both and said, "How about you gentlemen move your illegally parked vehicles out of the center turn lane and find someplace else to load your items. I really wanted to write a ticket today, so it looks like I will be the only one leaving here disappointed."

The three of us shook hands, and with all of us wearing smiles, we returned to our respective vehicles and cleared the highway. I loved my job, and some days were better than others.

Burglar on the Roof

My last three years on the highway patrol were spent as the traffic operations lieutenant over all the Truckee Meadows (Reno/Sparks area) and North Lake Tahoe. My main job was to supervise six sergeants and sixty-five troopers in the second-largest city in Nevada. With a captain who liked to hand out assignments, no secretary, numerous daily phone calls and messages to answer, planning with other agencies for special events in the area, unending paperwork, and handling the unexpected things that filled every day, getting out of the office was nearly impossible. When I did get a chance to get out of the office and work the highway for a few hours, I took it and I loved it.

One morning at about 12:30 a.m., I was on Sun Valley Boulevard (also known as Nevada State Route 443) when my dispatch center called and asked if I could assist a Washoe County deputy on a burglary call. Dispatch gave me the address and advised that a woman had reported one or more people walking around on the metal roof of her home. Home alone, the poor lady was scared out of her mind, and dispatch was going to keep her on the phone until we arrived.

I was two minutes away from the call, and the deputy I was to assist was five minutes behind me. In rural Nevada, it certainly wasn't unusual to get called to back up another agency and get to the scene long before they arrived, but it was less likely in a large city like Reno where each agency had several officers working each shift. The fact that the Washoe County Sheriff's Office called us for assistance probably meant everyone else was busy.

There are certain calls where you want to arrive in a hurry, but you wouldn't use lights and sirens, and this was one. If there was a guy (or guys) walking around on top of this scared lady's roof, I didn't want to let them know I was coming. I wanted to catch them up there and not let them escape into the night.

It was a dark night with no moon, and I was creeping through the neighborhood looking for the address when I saw movement on top of a mobile home. Without confirming the address, I knew I had found the right house. When I turned on my spotlight and focused it onto the roof of the house, the single culprit was readily identified.

I don't blame the poor woman for being scared because the racket the invader was making dancing around on the metal roof would wake the dead. I took no immediate action and waited in my patrol car for the deputy to arrive so he could see the burglar for himself. However, I did tell dispatch to inform the terrified woman that her intruder was one of the biggest mule deer bucks I had seen in a long time. It had four points on one side, five on the other, and had to weigh over two hundred pounds.

As soon as the deputy arrived, we had a good laugh and walked up to the mobile home. After waving our arms and yelling at the poor muley, he jumped off with such ease and grace we wondered why he hadn't done it sooner. He certainly hadn't been trapped up there, leaving one to wonder what had possessed him to get up there in the first place and stay for so long.

Afterward, we met with the woman who was very relieved and quite pleased that we had come to save her life and solve the "Case of the Wayward Buck."

I Thought I Could Drive

Every experienced driver has been passed on a highway by a state police patrol car going somewhere in a hurry. When I first became a state trooper, I figured that I would be driving fast occasionally, and I was quite surprised to learn that I would do so numerous times a day.

In the academy, we completed an Emergency Vehicle Operations Course (EVOC) where we learned basic non-emergency vehicle skills, skid control, pursuit driving, winter driving, and how to push cars to their limits on cornering, but all were taught at slow to moderate speeds.

On my first day driving a patrol car, I broke 100 miles per hour for the first time. I was sure I would be suffering a cataclysmic death at any moment. My training officer seated beside me screaming "faster, faster, or you're never going to catch him" did not make the situation any less stressful. I had a death grip on the steering wheel, broke into a nervous sweat, and knew there was no way I was going to remove either hand from the steering wheel to answer or make a call on the radio. Before long, it became second nature to drive fast, and traveling more than 100 miles per hour while talking on the radio and jotting down notes was no big deal.

The first ten years of my career, I attended several driving courses and drove a couple of hundred thousand miles in all types of weather, from hot summers in the desert to snowy, cold winters at Lake Tahoe. All in all, I was a little cocky and thought myself a darned good driver.

In 1995, I was a personnel sergeant at Nevada Highway Patrol Headquarters. The courts made numerous changes to physical agility testing requirements which caused problems and confusion for police and fire agencies across the nation. Suddenly, the standards we had been following for years were out the window, and no one seemed to have an answer as to how to move forward. The common answer from the federal government was, "We don't know what you can do, but you can no longer do what you have been doing."

As a result of the confusion, the North Carolina Highway Patrol hosted a Personnel Hiring Summit and invited all state police agencies to attend. When I explained the current predicament to my chief, he told me to attend the seminar.

The four-day hiring summit was being held on Tuesday through Friday at the Highway Patrol Academy in Raleigh. To save money, the clerical staff that arranged my flight from Reno to Raleigh chose to have me fly on a weekday rather than a weekend, so I arrived on Friday, four days prior to the event. I was not happy with the choice to arrive in Raleigh so early, but missing the seminar was not an option.

When I arrived at the Raleigh airport, I contacted the North Carolina Highway Patrol who sent a sergeant to pick me up. The sergeant and I rode around the city for a couple of hours and had dinner together before he took me to my room. We arrived at the academy where the sergeant gave me keys to a brand-new unmarked Ford Mustang, a gas card to fill it up with, and keys to the locked academy gate so that I could come and go as I pleased. What I thought was going to be a long, quiet, and boring four days turned into sightseeing and experiencing a new state.

Thirty-nine state police agencies attended the very informative summit. It was a lot of fun to spend time with so many of my colleagues. On Friday afternoon, North Carolina Highway Patrol Colonel Robert Barefoot put on a catered barbecue, and all of us were offered a ride in a department helicopter and in a pursuit vehicle on their high-speed track.

The helicopter ride around Raleigh was wonderful, and I would have easily done it twice, but the same can't be said for the ride in the pursuit car. The narrow, two-lane, high-speed course was several miles long with numerous sharp turns, and portions of it were lined with things that few Nevada troopers ever see—trees.

I was selected to ride in a white pursuit vehicle operated by a highway patrol driving instructor. The black vehicle we were to chase was also being driven by an instructor and had one of my seminar counterparts as a passenger. When it was time to go, I climbed into the passenger seat, strapped myself into a four-point harness, smiled at the highway patrol driving instructor seated behind the steering wheel, and said, "I am looking forward to this!"

The instructor smiled back, nodded, and said, "Let's go then."

The black car took off, and my driver mashed the gas pedal to the floor. Traveling at well over 100 miles per hour in mere seconds, we careened down the track less than a car length from the rear bumper of the black vehicle. My smile disappeared in a hurry as we approached a 90-degree left turn. Hanging on for dear life with my right foot tapping the floorboard searching for the brake pedal that didn't exist, we shot around the turn at a speed faster than any vehicle should be able to. The next hairpin turn to the right was a repeat of the first but lined with trees. Throughout the entire demonstration I was convinced I was going to die. After pursuing the lead vehicle several miles around the entire track, we finally slid to a stop back where we had begun.

The instructor smiled and said, "Do you want to go again?"

"No, sir!" I said. "I do not want to go again, and it's lucky for you that I am not armed!"

I attended numerous driving courses during my career, and I am sure that when it came to driving a patrol car on ice and snow-covered highways, few North Carolina troopers could compare. But when it came to pursuing another vehicle at ridiculously high speeds on a skinny, two-lane, tree-lined highway, compared to these men I was totally inept.

Pet Emergency

Late one Friday evening, I was on patrol on Sparks Boulevard just north of I-80 when I observed a passenger car on the east side of the road with its emergency flashers on. I advised dispatch of the stop and pulled in behind what appeared to be an empty, running car with its headlights on. As I got even with the driver's door, I spotted a lady sitting on the curb in front of the car. She was rocking back and forth, crying, and cradling an injured Labrador retriever in her arms. It was apparent from the roadway marks and blood that the dog had recently been hit by a car.

"Is that dog yours?" I asked.

"Yes, it is," she said. "He got out of the yard, so I went looking for him, and I just found him. He must have gotten hit."

"It appears so," I said.

Being a rural trooper for thirteen years, I had assessed injuries and provided care to more people than I care to count while waiting for an ambulance to arrive, so I proceeded to check out the dog. I had no idea how to check for a doggy pulse nor how to take a blood-pressure reading like I would on a person, so I counted respirations, checked its level of alertness, and gave the lady a towel from my trunk to apply pressure to its bleeding wounds.

"There is an animal hospital emergency room clear across town in south Reno that is open twenty-four hours a day," I told her. "Are you interested in getting your dog there for care?"

"Oh, that would be wonderful," she said.

"Is there someone I can call for you that could help you do that?" I asked.

"No one that could be here soon," she cried.

As the urban traffic lieutenant that night, I had plenty of time to transport an injured Lab to the doggy hospital. Sometimes it was good to be the boss. Plus, I had weenie dogs at home, and I loved them dearly. I could certainly appreciate what this poor lady was going through.

I grabbed one of the yellow, plastic emergency blankets I carried in my trunk and placed it on my backseat. After loading the lady and her bloody Lab, I contacted Reno dispatch.

"Reno, 3067."

"3067."

"I will be transporting an injured dog and its owner, a WFA (white female adult) to the Pet Emergency Hospital in south Reno. Beginning mileage is 40,527.08. Would you contact the hospital and advise that we are en route with a seriously injured patient."

There was very little traffic that late at night on I-80, so I lit the car up with overhead red and blue flashing emergency lights, wig-wag bright headlights, and proceeded south. Knowing that we were getting there a little faster brought a brief smile to the worried lady's face which was nice to see.

Like many of the services troopers perform, I never learned the outcome. It would have been nice had the lady contacted me to let me know if the dog survived, but people's lives are busy, and I certainly never expected it.

This Should Be Someone Else's Job

In 1995 my wife Janelle decided to open a water garden business at our home in Carson City. Within three years we had moved Oasis Water Gardens to a small retail location in Sparks, and two years later to a 5,000-square-foot storefront with a large outdoor area and six full-time employees. We cleaned, repaired, built, and serviced all types of outdoor aquatic features from small home fishponds to large lakes. We raised water plants, imported koi fish from Japan, built pond filters, and sold everything a pond owner/builder could possibly need from construction materials to fish medicine.

Janelle and I studied very hard over the years and turned Oasis Water Gardens into a very successful business. The only problem was that the business (technically my wife's) was labor intensive, and for six years I was both a highway patrol lieutenant and a pond guy until I retired in 2001. We both worked very hard, and days off were few and far between.

One day, I was working at the store and asked our young employee, Lisa, to clean the filters on the koi tanks. Cleaning fish filters is a smelly, dirty affair and not a job anyone liked to do, so my request was met with resistance.

"That shouldn't be my job," Lisa said. "That should be someone else's job!"

I looked at Lisa and said, "Lisa, I know exactly how you feel. Just last week I was called to a fatal traffic accident in Hazen, Nevada."

I briefly explained to Lisa how the accident happened. A motorcycle was making a left turn into the bar parking lot and was struck in the rear by a car which left the scene. The motorcycle was pushed across the center line directly into the path of a westbound commercial tractor/trailer, killing the motorcycle driver instantly. The body of the driver was found in the roadway where the collision occurred. What was left of the motorcycle got wrapped up in the rear dual axles of the semi-trailer and burst into flames. The semi-trailer with motorcycle underneath stopped about 150 feet down the highway where the whole mess continued to burn. Thinking there was only one man killed, imagine our surprise when the trailer fire was extinguished and we saw the burned remains of a woman. Apparently, the woman had been a passenger on the back of the motorcycle when it was hit.

In rural Nevada, the funeral wagon arriving at an accident scene is often driven by an old person who is quite useless at retrieving and loading bodies for transport without help, as was the case that day. Both troopers were busy investigating and documenting the accident scene, so I put on a pair of rubber gloves and crawled under the rear end of the semi-trailer to remove the body of the well-cooked woman.

"So, Lisa, without going into any gorier details, I will tell you that I was thinking the same thing that you are thinking right now. This shouldn't be my job; this should be someone else's job! Now, go clean the fish filters!"

As a lieutenant, when I did show up at serious accidents or incidents, I would ask the trooper investigating what they needed me to do, and I would help. Well-trained professional troopers know their jobs and are seldom in need of supervision, so I found it best to stay out of their way. However, that was one day I wished that I hadn't shown up at all.

The Art of Tracking

I was just finishing up my shift on a cold winter's night and headed to my Carson City home when dispatch called with a change of plans. A trooper assigned to the Hawthorne District had just arrested a local man for driving under the influence on US 95, three miles north of the town of Luning. The trooper had handcuffed the drunk and strapped him into the front seat of his patrol car. While the trooper was away from his car dealing with the passenger of the vehicle, the prisoner managed to free himself and disappear into the desert. I was 133 miles away but responded like we always did, driving far and fast.

Luning, Nevada is a tiny unincorporated area of Mineral County located twenty miles south of Hawthorne, four miles north of Mina, and thirty-two miles south of Gabbs. Other than these three populated areas (two of them barely), the nearest towns of any size were Fallon (ninety-six miles to the north) and Tonopah (eighty miles to the south). You can see why having a handcuffed prisoner on the loose, far from anyone and anywhere on a cold winter's night, could be a problem. The only saving grace was that we knew who the man was and that he was one of the eighty-seven documented residents of Luning.

I arrived on scene and met with the trooper and the one Mineral County deputy sent to assist. The passenger had been taken home, and the three of us attempted to locate the escaped prisoner. I had a four-wheel-drive patrol car, so driving into the desert was no problem, but trying to follow footprints across a desert comprised of more rock than sand on a dark night was proving impossible. After several frustratingly fruitless hours of searching the desert, we checked the man's residence in Luning with no results, so we called it a night. The next day, the still-handcuffed prisoner sobered up and called and asked if the trooper could pick him up at his home. The trooper was happy to oblige him, and thankfully he was alright.

Three weeks later, I was in the town of Fernley when I was called to assist one of my troopers who was in pursuit of a vehicle on I-80. The trooper had tried to stop a vehicle, but the driver had no intention of stopping. The trooper chased the car toward Reno, when the driver left the freeway in a hurry and drove down several dirt roads and stopped right on the edge of the Truckee River. The man, in his forties, ran from the vehicle into the tall brush and disappeared. A few minutes later, the trooper stopped behind the car and found an older woman passenger sitting in the right-front seat. On the seat next to the woman was an empty holster and an empty box of .38-caliber bullets.

I arrived a short time later and met with the trooper to discuss what turned out to be a strange situation. It was late in the afternoon, the vehicle had been reported stolen in Las Vegas, the now armed and unknown driver was somewhere in the weeds along the river, and the woman left sitting in the car claimed to be the escaped driver's mother. The mother wouldn't identify herself, wouldn't give us the name of her proclaimed son, and seemed quite content to sit there forever knowing he would not be coming back.

We knew we had a bad guy on the run, and the first step in capturing him would be to set up a perimeter. Though a couple of troopers were on their way to assist, it would require many more officers than we could ever get on short notice. This large, brushy, swampy area with tons of cover went on for miles. From here, this guy could go into the mountains north or south, move along the river east or west, hide for an eternity, or work his way back to the interstate and hitch a ride. Knowing daylight would be gone in an hour or two, and unable to leave the woman alone in a stolen car, only one of us would be able to try and track this guy down. One officer following an armed guy into the weeds by himself is something you see on television, but in real life it is a great way for an officer to die. What to do?

My first thought was to contact the Washoe County Sheriff's Office and ask for their helicopter to respond. We were twenty miles east of Reno, and locating the armed guy from the air seemed like a good idea. I contacted the Washoe County Sheriff's Office and made my request, only to be turned down by the watch commander who said, "Right now your culprit is only wanted for possession of a stolen vehicle. Other than that, we have no idea who he is or what other crimes he might be wanted for."

"Well, we don't know who he is," I said, "but as of now he is wanted for several traffic violations, including eluding, he appears to be armed with a .38-caliber handgun, he left his dear old mother sitting in a stolen car, and he escaped into the tall weeds along the Truckee River. Commander, do you really believe that this guy, whoever he is, wouldn't have an extensive criminal record?"

"I'm sorry," he said. "But without more information we won't be able to respond."

Two other troopers arrived and took care of mom and the car while the two of us stayed on binoculars, looking for any movement until sundown ended the hunt. Mom was identified and booked into the county jail for possession of a stolen vehicle. I assigned extra patrol to that area for the remainder of the night in case the guy came crawling out of the weeds and tried to catch a ride on the interstate. The guy that got away was indeed the woman's son and was identified as an escapee from a Washington State prison. Word must have gotten around because the next day I received a call from the Washoe County sheriff apologizing for the actions of his command officer. I was assured that if I ever needed the helicopter again, it would be sent.

A week or two later, I was advised that two of the troopers in my district were looking for an individual in the desert and had failed to locate him. Though we didn't have the manpower or daylight to safely search for the armed individual, it was apparent that we state troopers were quite inept at tracking and locating people in the deserts and mountains we called home.

A good friend of mine, John Coleman, was a warden with the Nevada Department of Corrections. John was an expert in the field of man tracking, taught classes on the subject, and oversaw a team of correctional officers used for that purpose, which included his son John. John agreed to teach us a basic class and gave me a list of items for each of us to bring to class, including a ski pole with several rubber bands around the tip. Three weeks later, two sergeants, eight troopers, and I started our two-day class in the town of Fernley. The first day was spent in a classroom, and the second day in a remote desert canyon six miles north of Wadsworth, Nevada.

One would think that following a person's tracks across most terrains would be basic common sense and not brain surgery, but it truly is a science. While we as students were mostly concerned with locating escaped suspects, we quickly learned that man-tracking skills are very useful in locating lost individuals, seniors with dementia, young or special needs children who have wandered away, and retracing one's own steps should you find yourself lost in the outdoors.

In the classroom, we learned the basics of man tracking. Applying these principles can often identify an individual's direction of travel, which can greatly reduce the size of an area to be searched. We learned how to identify, size, photograph, sketch, and analyze shoe patterns and footprints. Next came analyzing and measuring a person's stride. Was the individual walking, running, jumping, or limping? Next came instruction on the use of our ski poles. We placed the tip of the ski pole at the heel of the next footprint and moved the rubber band to the toe of the preceding print. This shows a measurement of the stride of the person you are following and exactly where the next print should be. In rough terrain, a hard-to-find print can be identified by a broken twig, an overturned leaf, rock, pebble, or anything else that appears out of the ordinary.

Not all tracks are obvious and can easily be lost when the type of terrain changes to rock or another hard surface, so we were taught to look for "track traps" in areas of wet dirt, dust, sand, or any other surface condition that would preserve a print. The last identified track should always be marked before searching for the next. It can be a tedious task, so working with a partner is a plus.

Next came lighting and how it can affect the ability to track. I taught traffic accident investigation for many years which included identifying the many different types of skid and scuff marks that can be left by the tires of a vehicle. Tire marks, just like tracks, can be very difficult to see under certain conditions depending on the time of day, lighting, and the brightness or angle of the sun. Using a light on the track from a different angle or direction will often highlight an otherwise invisible print.

For eight hours on day two, we tracked each other across the desert, along a creek, and into the mountains in what could be described as a giant game of hide and seek for men. It was a great day and a lot of fun. Though we were given only a basic course in man tracking, all of us in attendance greatly sharpened our skills and gained confidence in our ability to track someone down.

What was very apparent by the end of the day is that both our instructors were light-years ahead of us in both training and experience, leaving me in awe at their abilities. In fact, I left there feeling a little sorry for any prison inmates trying to escape from these two officers on foot because their chances of getting away were somewhere between slim and none.

Who's the Bigger Idiot?

One day I was in Colonel Hood's office when I looked up and saw a photograph of a younger Sergeant Hood working crowd control at a large protest. In the photo, he was standing directly next to, and turning away from, an older male protester. I asked if the man with him in the photo was the infamous "Feces Man" from the Nevada Test Site, and Colonel Hood said that it was.

The Nevada Test Site (NTS) is located 65 miles northwest of Las Vegas and was established on January 11, 1951 for the testing of nuclear devices. It covers approximately 1,360 square miles of desert and mountainous terrain. Over 1,000 nuclear weapons tests were detonated at the NTS over four decades, with mushroom clouds commonly visible over 100 miles away. Throughout those four decades, over 500 anti-nuclear protests were held at the Nevada Test Site, involving tens of thousands of participants, resulting in over 15,000 arrests.

"Feces Man" was a regular at the NTS protest events and was very well-known among law enforcement personnel in Nevada. Very few in law enforcement had ever met him, and even fewer had been forced to deal with him, but in a small state like Nevada, his exploits were the topic of conversation at every cop coffee break south to north. How did Feces Man earn his moniker? At every protest, he paraded around completely naked, covered head to toe in human excrement. Yes, he was arrested every time, and yes, it was usually the troopers with the lowest seniority who had the displeasure of arresting him, handcuffing him, and transporting him to the temporary jail.

After studying the photograph for a few moments, and noticing the crazy look in Feces Man's eyes and the look of disgust on then Sergeant Hood's face, I asked Colonel Hood, "Do you remember what you were thinking when this photo was snapped?"

Colonel Hood said, "The moment that photo was taken, I was thinking to myself, who was the bigger idiot: Feces Man, for running around naked covered head to toe in human waste, or me, having just spent several minutes trying to reason with a man running around naked, covered head to toe in human waste?"

The lesson I took to heart as a state trooper was don't try to reason with unreasonable people like Feces Man, druggies, and drunks.

Y2K

It was the night of December 31, 1999. While people debated whether the new millennium actually began January 1, 2000 or January 1, 2001, as far as computers were concerned, the big date the world had to be concerned about was when their internal clocks failed to turn to the year 2000.

The Y2K bug, also called the Millennium Bug, was predicted to create havoc in computers around the world. The fear was that many computer programs, developed in the 1900s, would not recognize the year 2000. Large computer mainframe systems and computer programs associated with government agencies, financial institutions, and utilities around the world would shut down resulting in mass chaos. People's bank accounts would disappear, elevators would stop, computerized car engines would die, mass transportation systems would fail, and life as we knew it would cease to exist.

Hundreds of billions of dollars were spent around the world in preparation for the big day. Computer programmers worked around the clock preparing. Everyone who could afford a generator bought one (or two) and stocked up on fuel. I didn't have the extra money to go out and buy a generator, but I was wondering what I was going to do with the food in my refrigerator when the power went out at midnight.

So, what did Y2K mean for me, you ask? Well, it was another New Year's Eve spent in a patrol car, just like the twenty New Year's Eves prior to this one. I had never had one off, and even if I had, no one was going to invite a highway patrol lieutenant over to spoil the party at their house, so I worked.

I was the only highway patrol lieutenant working the road in the Reno/Carson City/Lake Tahoe area, so all I had to do was drive around and supervise a handful of sergeants and a couple dozen troopers who also seldom had New Year's Eve off. How hard could that be, you ask. Well, it was easy until around 9:45 p.m.

I was northbound on US 395, just south of Carson City at the intersection with Topsy Lane, when I noticed a patrol car with its overhead lights on in the travel lane directly in front of me. This area was rural at the time with no major shopping centers, unlike today. I could tell from the emergency lights on the patrol car that it belonged to a different agency. As I pulled to a stop behind the patrol car, I was met by a Washoe Tribal Police officer.

"Lieutenant, I'm glad you're here," he said. "You need to see this."

The officer led me around his patrol car where lying directly in front of it, in the glow of the headlights, was the deceased body of a teenage girl. There were no cars and no witnesses—just the dead girl, the tribal officer, and me. It was apparent from the eerie, deserted scene that this young lady could not have been there very long. What on earth had happened to this young lady? Why was she alone? Had she been the victim of a hit and run? Had she been a pedestrian crossing the highway and struck by a car? Had she been murdered? Had she been killed somewhere else and dumped here? So many questions. And where to begin?

I contacted my dispatch center and advised them of my location and situation. I asked that she request the Carson City Sheriff's Office and coroner to respond, along with the nearest NHP sergeant and trooper. Then the tribal officer and I went about trying to solve this puzzle.

The young lady had suffered major head injuries, which is a very common fatal injury in many types of motor vehicle accidents. It wasn't the injuries she'd received, but the injuries she hadn't received that had me stumped.

During my studies at the Northwestern University Traffic Institute, I'd taken classes on vehicle occupant placement (how to determine where occupants had been seated in a vehicle prior to ejection) and vehicle/pedestrian collisions and related injuries. I'd learned that there are three phases to a vehicle/pedestrian collision. The first phase is "initial contact," during which the pedestrian wraps around or is carried by the striking vehicle. The second phase is "trajectory," which are the actions of the pedestrian as they separate from the vehicle and move toward the ground. The third phase is "ground contact," which includes the actions of the pedestrian from first contact with the ground until they come to rest

In vehicle/pedestrian collisions, the investigator looks at physical evidence at the site, including dents on the vehicle and broken parts, blood stains and blood trails, shoe scuff marks on the roadway surface, final position of rest of the vehicle and the victim, measurement of tire marks, and pedestrian injuries. If you think about a direct hit between a moving motor vehicle and a pedestrian, you will realize that all, or least a part, of the pedestrian is going to instantly accelerate and match the speed of the striking vehicle. This action commonly results in major injuries and one or more broken bones to the pedestrian's leg(s).

I could go on for days regarding the dynamics involved in vehicle/pedestrian collisions, but suffice it to say that this night nothing was adding up. No witnesses, no striking vehicle, no broken vehicle parts, no tire marks, and a relatively short blood trail. The major clue for me that the young woman had not been struck by a vehicle was the lack of any apparent injuries to her legs.

The highway patrol trooper and sergeant arrived, and in good lieutenant fashion I turned the investigation over to them. Later that evening, I was advised of what had taken place. About two hours after the young woman's body was found, the Carson City Sheriff's Office received a call from two sets of parents who advised that their children had been involved in an incident earlier in the evening on US 395, in which a friend of theirs had been injured. The story was that the young woman was sitting on her boyfriend's lap in the front passenger seat, and they began arguing. The intoxicated young woman allegedly said she was going to jump out of the car. She opened the door and either jumped or fell or was pushed out onto the highway. The kids pulled over, went back to look at her, saw that she was severely injured, got scared, and drove off. As we arrived and worked the scene, the three kids sat in their darkened car on a dirt road, where they had a view of the scene and watched the goings on before heading home to tell their parents what had occurred.

I hate to leave you with an unfinished story, but I never learned the outcome of this case. Short of direct testimony from witnesses, it would have been very difficult or impossible to prove whether the young lady jumped, fell, or was pushed. From the injuries, I would guess that the young woman's death was very quick, but to leave the scene of an accident, drive off, and not try to get her medical help is a felony in our state and should have been enough to land the driver, if not all of them, in hot water.

You're Lying to the Public

S treet Vibrations is a large motorcycle festival held in Reno each year from the last Wednesday through Sunday of September. Well over 35,000 riders converge on the city and participate in metal music concerts, live entertainment, and poker runs where they're cruising around Lake Tahoe and the Carson City, Virginia City, and Reno highways. Generally, it is a busy time for the highway patrol troopers in the area, and September of 2001 was no different.

As the Reno/North Lake Tahoe highway patrol commander, I was praying that all would go well and there would be few problems. The first two days were quiet, but my luck didn't last. Friday afternoon on US 395 south of Reno, the clouds opened and poured rain. Commuter traffic between Carson City and Reno was always a problem on Friday afternoons, but throw in a rainstorm and thousands of motorcycles running around and it soon became a mess.

I had a speaker in my office where I could monitor all radio traffic between dispatch and the troopers and stay apprised of all that was going on in the Reno area. At 5:03 p.m. I heard the dispatcher direct a trooper to an injury accident involving a tow truck and a motorcycle on US 395 south at Andrew Lane. The accident was blocking both northbound lanes, and all northbound commuter traffic from Carson City was stopped. Swing-shift Sergeant Dan Luke was in the office at the time and advised me that he was headed down to the accident.

About ten minutes later, another trooper arrived on scene and

200

advised that a motorcyclist was injured, pinned under the tow truck, and was awaiting extrication by Reno Fire.

After hearing that news, it was time for me to head there as well. I left the highway patrol office and was walking toward my car in the parking lot when I noticed Sgt. Luke sitting in his patrol car talking on his cell phone. He should have been arriving at the wreck about then and had not even left the office. As I approached his patrol car, he rolled down the driver's window. It was clear that Sgt. Luke was speaking to someone of authority, as anyone else would have been put off until after the accident situation was under control.

Sgt. Luke said, "No, sir. Yes, sir. No, sir. Yes, sir," and without a goodbye ended the call.

"Who was that, Dan?" I asked.

For the purposes of this story, we will call this new upper-level commander, who had absolutely no previous experience as a state trooper, "The Big Boss."

"That was The Big Boss," Sgt. Luke replied.

"Well, what's he doing calling you?" I asked. "He should have been talking to me!"

"I don't know," Dan replied. "But he is stuck in traffic at the accident scene on his way home from Carson City, and he is not happy!"

I was far from happy myself. This man should have called me on the phone to discuss the situation, not my sergeant, thereby delaying him from responding to a situation that desperately needed his attention.

I jumped into my patrol car, and Sgt. Luke and I left the office parking lot. While making my way to the accident scene, one of my troopers advised dispatch over the radio that The Big Boss wanted us to reroute northbound stopped traffic back over Mt. Rose. I was not about to tell dispatch over the radio that The Big Boss's request was just about the stupidest idea I had heard in twenty-five years of traffic control, so I called her on my cell phone and advised her to keep that idiotic idea to herself until I got to the scene and assessed the situation.

Why was it a stupid idea? Well, let me explain:

1. To turn around several thousand cars, all stopped on one half of a four-lane highway and head them in another direction is at best difficult, especially in a raging rainstorm, and doing so would take hours. The now open I-580 freeway was years from completion, so there were only two other highways to, as The Big Boss requested, reroute traffic on.

2. Both ridiculous options required sending all traffic twenty miles in the opposite direction right back through the center of downtown Carson City.

Option One: From downtown Carson City, redirected traffic would drive fourteen miles up US 50 to Spooner Summit, a good four-lane highway, then they would be dumped onto State Route 28, a two-lane, very slow road that hugs and winds around the northern shore of Lake Tahoe for another thirteen miles to Incline Village. State Route 431 from Incline Village to Reno is another thirty-six miles of steep, windy, two-lane highway. So, this entire rerouted trip would be a total of eighty-three miles, most of which were on highways not designed for that much traffic, with or without rain.

Option Two: Suffice it to say that "rerouting" traffic over the mountains through Virginia City was a worse idea than Option One.

3: As soon as the motorcyclist was extricated from under the tow truck, loaded onto CareFlight, and whisked away to the hospital (which would only take a matter of minutes), traffic would begin moving again.

Luckily for me, when I arrived at the scene The Big Boss was gone and had driven right through the middle of the closed scene, much to the ire of the firemen who were holding a cleared landing zone for CareFlight. I thought I was done with The Big Boss for the night, but was I wrong.

CareFlight took off with the patient, traffic was moving (albeit slowly), and several local television news crews were reporting on the evening news live from the scene. My PIO (Public Information Officer) whose job was to handle the media was giving interviews and hard at it while the rest of the troopers were attending to business.

Suddenly, my cell phone rang, and dispatch said, "Lieutenant Raabe, The Big Boss is on the line, and I am patching him through to you."

"Yes, sir," I answered.

In an angry tone, The Big Boss said, "Lieutenant Raabe, why are you lying to the public?"

"What do you mean? How am I lying to the public, sir?"

"Your trooper is on the television telling everyone that no one died in that accident, and I know that someone did."

"Hold on, sir."

I immediately turned to a couple of the troopers who were working the accident and asked them if anyone had died in this event. Both replied that they weren't aware of any fatalities.

"Sir, according to the troopers handling this accident, there are only serious injuries at this time. No one has died."

"Lieutenant Raabe, I know someone died in that wreck because I was told so before I left my office in Carson City." Then he screamed into the phone, "Quit lying to the public and do your job right!"

Just like his previous call to Sgt. Luke, the line went dead without so much as a goodbye. Lucky for me, he said nothing about his advice to my trooper to reroute traffic.

I called my dispatch center and advised them to send a trooper to the Renown Hospital Trauma Center immediately and verify whether the injured person from this accident was still alive.

About fifteen minutes later, dispatch called and informed me that a trooper had just cleared the emergency room and reported that the motorcyclist from the accident was still alive.

At this point, I was at a loss and didn't know what to think. The Big Boss was adamant that he had been told earlier that someone had died in this accident before he left his office. My new boss had called me a liar, screamed at me to do my job right, and then hung up on me.

Then I got an idea.

I called dispatch back and asked, "Has anyone died in an accident today in our area?"

"Yes, Lieutenant Raabe," she said. "We had a bicyclist killed on US 50 at Spooner Summit a couple of hours ago."

I did not call The Big Boss back to try to explain the situation, as it would have been futile, and the last thing I wanted to do was speak to that man again, ever!

Unfortunately, I wasn't that lucky. And to say my career went downhill after this event and several others over the course of the next few months would be an understatement.

The Devil Made Me Do It

As lieutenant of traffic operations over the Reno Urban District, most of my time was spent behind the desk in my Reno office, but since I lived thirty miles south in Carson City, I had an hour or two every day to patrol US 395, which I enjoyed.

US 395 between Reno and Carson City was the busiest, most dangerous stretch of highway in all northern Nevada. It consisted of two northbound lanes, two southbound lanes, and a center turn lane stuffed with commuter traffic, much of it running through business districts and residential areas with numerous side streets and private driveways. Commuters wanted to pass through as fast as they could and get to work, while people who lived and worked in the area wanted to get in and out of their driveways and side streets without getting killed!

One Saturday afternoon, I pulled a car over just south of Reno at the entrance to a western wear store. I approached the car, and while conversing with the driver, I observed an older cowboy exit the store and head directly toward me. He appeared to me to have "the walk." You know, the walk that implies unhappiness, demonstrates purpose, and results in confrontation.

When the man got close enough to shout at me, he said, "Hey, I need to talk to you right now!"

My immediate concern was with the traffic stop I had just made, so I asked the cowboy, "Sir, is this an emergency? If not, you will have to wait until I finish this traffic stop and then you will have my undivided attention."

This request didn't appear to make him any happier, but he stood there for about ten minutes as I issued a citation and concluded my stop. As soon as I released the violator, I approached the cowboy who said, "Don't you know that you are not allowed to stop cars right in front of my business?"

"Obviously not," I answered.

"Well, it's bad for my business, and all of you cops need to know that it is unacceptable."

"Well, sir," I responded, "the entire traffic stop was conducted on highway right-of-way, and at no time was I on your property."

"It doesn't matter," he said. "You were blocking a portion of my driveway."

"Sir, as you know, this is a very busy, dangerous stretch of highway with limited places to stop traffic safely. We do our best to not disrupt anyone's business, but my safety and that of all troopers working this area supersedes the very occasional, ten-minute disruption any business along this route might experience."

"I don't care about any of that," the cowboy said. "I am the owner, and you just cannot stop cars directly in front of my store."

"Quite often, even though we as officers might have a different idea, the violator chooses where to pull over," I explained.

"It doesn't matter who picks the spot as long as you make it happen anywhere but in front of my driveway."

"Well, sir, I am sorry," I said. "But the traffic stop was made on the highway right-of-way, and I cannot guarantee that I or any other trooper will not make a traffic stop here in the future."

Clearly not happy with my answer and more upset than ever, he stated, "I demand to have the phone number of the person that is in charge of this area right now, so I can straighten this out."

I gave him the phone number he demanded and returned to my patrol car, and he returned to his business. I know I shouldn't have done it, but I did. I'm sure he never noticed the bars on the points of my collar or the small print on my badge that said lieutenant, so I returned to my patrol car and waited for his call.

The phone rang a few minutes later, and I answered, "Nevada Highway Patrol, this is Lieutenant Raabe."

"Is this the highway patrol boss in charge of Reno?" the man asked.

"Yes, sir, it is," I said. "I am the commander over the Reno area. I am still in my patrol car in front of your business, and the answer is still the same."

I am quite proud of my record as a state trooper, as I never had one sustained complaint from the motoring public or citizen over the course of my entire career, but this was a day I deserved one. For the next few days, I waited for the call from the captain regarding the complaint from the western wear guy, but it never came. I was right about being able to stop vehicles in that exact spot, but wrong to give the guy my phone number. I guess the devil made me do it.

Too Close for This Dad

I was so fortunate to have my oldest son, Trooper Tim Raabe, follow in my footsteps. Following a five-year enlistment in the United States Air Force, Tim returned home to Nevada, attended college for two years, and graduated from the Western Nevada Police Academy in 2002. Tim began his law enforcement career as a police officer for the Winnemucca Police Department. Two years later, he became a Nevada Highway Patrol trooper assigned to the Winnemucca District. I was assigned to the same district as a trooper from 1980 until 1993, so when my son calls and shares his experiences with his dear old dad, I can certainly relate to his day-to-day experiences, including the dangers of working in a rural district.

In most departments, when an officer asks dispatch for a cover unit or backup, officers can show up in minutes. When rural troopers working alone in the expansive deserts of the American West call for backup, the situation is usually resolved one way or another, good or bad, before help arrives. I loved my job patrolling the desert and realized the dangers, but having your son out there every day is worrisome. However, this is the story of an incident that took place on a very rare day when Tim was not alone. Had he been so, he very possibly would not be alive today.

On October 23, 2013, the Nevada State Police, accompanied by a few officers from other local departments, were working highway interdiction on I-80 just west of the town of Battle Mountain. The interdiction method used to stop potential drug smugglers and wanted felons was commonly referred as the "Highway Hoax." The Highway Hoax involves placing large signs beside the interstate in the middle of the desert warning drivers of a drug checkpoint ahead. The funny thing is that the checkpoint is a ruse. The signs are deliberately placed prior to an off-ramp, near a highway crossover and a rise in the terrain that prevents drivers from seeing down the road. This warning instills fear in most criminals and drug smugglers, prompting them to exit the highway immediately. When doing so, most don't come to a complete stop at the stop sign at the bottom of the remote off-ramp, or even better, they change directions by illegally crossing the freeway median to avoid the fake checkpoint. Officers watch for these frequent violations from a distance, giving them the legal authority to stop the vehicle.

At 2:50 p.m., a man driving a gray Nissan Altima passed the checkpoint warning sign and promptly took the 222-mile exit, rolling through the stop sign at the bottom of the ramp. Humboldt County Deputy Chris Leninger, one of the officers assigned to the team, relayed the stop sign violation information to Winnemucca Police Officer Elizabeth Hill. The suspect's vehicle crossed under the freeway and re-entered I-80 westbound. Officer Hill, assisted by Nevada State Police Detective Sergeant Jason Franklin, made a traffic stop on the Nissan at mile marker 222 for the stop sign violation.

Officer Hill approached the vehicle and contacted the driver who produced a New York driver's license identifying himself as John Dellafiora along with a Hertz car rental agreement. Officer Hill noticed that Dellafiora was acting strangely, licking his lips frequently, and avoiding eye contact. He appeared unsure of his location and was trying to use a map to describe his destination. Sergeant Franklin asked Dellafiora where he was coming from and where he was going, and his answers were contradictory and made little sense. Sergeant Franklin noticed a large black trash bag and a jacket spread out on the backseat, so he and Officer Hill decided to give Dellafiora a written warning for the stop sign and run Officer Hill's K-9, Duchess, around the vehicle to detect any odors of narcotics.

When Officer Hill returned to the car and asked Dellafiora to step from his vehicle, his behavior changed quickly from nervous to angry to confrontational. Dellafiora promptly rolled up his car window, started the engine, and drove off. Officer Hill jumped into her patrol car and followed Dellafiora westbound on I-80 and was soon joined in the pursuit by Hoax team members Trooper Raabe and Deputy Rochester. Officer Hill had vehicle problems, so Trooper Raabe, accompanied by his longtime Belgian Malinois and K-9 partner, Gripper, took over as the primary pursuit unit while Deputy Rochester dropped back to keep uninvolved vehicles from getting too close to the situation.

The pursuit proceeded for thirty-eight miles, never exceeding seventy-five miles per hour. Highway Patrol Lieutenant Greg Johnson and Trooper Chris Wirthen, not members of the Highway Hoax team but working in the same area, deployed spike strips at mile marker 194. The spike attempt was successful, and both the front and rear tires on the passenger side of the Nissan were flattened. Unable to continue, Dellafiora made a right turn, traveling the wrong direction onto the mile marker 194 westbound (Golconda) on-ramp with Trooper Raabe right on his tail.

The initial trooper in any pursuit is very busy. They must drive their own car safely, monitor the actions of the vehicle being pursued, watch all other traffic, watch the suspect's actions inside the vehicle, anticipate and plan for the possibility of turns and stops throughout the chase, continually relay information over the radio to dispatch and other units, decide on the best choice of weapon to use for the situation, and be ready to react to whatever happens.

Dellafiora brought the Nissan to an abrupt stop halfway up the on-ramp, and Tim, sensing a dangerous situation, stopped a few seconds later about three car-lengths behind him. While sliding to a stop, Tim saw the Nissan driver's door open, and Dellafiora began to get out. For a second or two, Tim thought he and Gripper would be chasing the man across the desert, but then he saw a semi-automatic rifle in the man's hands. Dellafiora took a position at the front of his vehicle and promptly began to fill the driver's-side windshield and other frontal areas of Tim's patrol car with bullets. Lying down across the front seat and dodging bullets, Tim had no way to retrieve his firearm and return fire.

In a matter of seconds, Officer Hill pulled her patrol car right next to Tim's. Hill immediately started receiving rounds through her front windshield and was peppered in the face with broken glass. Hill backed up in a hurry to a position behind Tim's patrol car, while Trooper Tanner arrived and positioned his patrol car offset behind Officer Hill's.

Dellafiora's semi-automatic rifle was later identified as an AR-10, which as demonstrated on Tim's patrol car, can put holes right through a ¼-inch steel plate push bumper, a dashboard, and the front engine compartment grill and firewall as if they were nothing. Bullets hitting all over the inside of Tim's car left him with only two options: stay inside and die, or get out and run.

Tim jumped from his patrol car and ran toward the rear of Officer Hill's car in a zig-zag pattern yelling *automatic rifle* to his fellow officers. Videos of the event show Dellafiora concentrating his gunfire at Tim as he ran with bullets whizzing right past his head and body. Tim tripped and fell, and several officers thought he had been hit by gunfire, but he got up in a hurry and continued his sprint to the rear of Officer Hill's car, arriving unscathed and lucky.

Trooper Tanner was in a better position than Tim and was able to return fire with his .40-caliber Sig Sauer duty weapon, striking Dellafiora in the upper left arm. Dellafiora, now wounded and reloading, kept ducking behind the level of his vehicle's roof and moved back and forth from the front driver and passenger sides of the vehicle for cover.

Other officers were now arriving and getting their patrol cars into position around the shooter, including Nevada State Police Detective John Dunckhorst, a member of the Highway Hoax team, and Humboldt County Deputy Lee Dove, who was on normal patrol when he got the call of a pursuit.

Detective Dunckhorst, armed with an AR-15 rifle, fired multiple rounds at Dellafiora. Deputy Dove fired two rounds from his duty pistol and then transitioned to his AR-15. While moving forward and firing, Dove put one bullet into Dellafiora's head, ending the threat to all. Dellafiora fell near the front of his vehicle, and seven officers, including Trooper Tim Raabe, approached Dellafiora to secure the scene and render aid. After handcuffing Dellafiora, he was pronounced dead at the scene.

Of immediate concern to Tim was his K-9 and best friend Gripper. They had worked together for years, and so many bullets had been shot into and through Tim's patrol car, that he was afraid that Gripper was dead. Tim approached the back door of his patrol car with dread and opened it. Gripper was alive and excited to see Tim, but when Gripper jumped into his arms, he saw the blood from Gripper's gunshot wounds. Tim's car was shot to hell and was now evidence, so upset and afraid for his friend, he loaded Gripper into another patrol car and headed to the veterinarians' office in Winnemucca. Gripper had received thirteen different wounds from bullet fragments. He underwent surgery and had eleven pieces of shrapnel removed, while two were left in place. Gripper returned to work after a couple of weeks of sick leave and bed rest and was quite happy to do so.

As a lieutenant, I supervised several troopers with K-9s, and it takes a special team to be successful. It is not always a good match between trooper and dog, but when you get the perfect combination, it's magic. I witnessed that magic years before, watching my good friend Trooper

212

Brent Harmon and his K-9, Katie. Tim and Gripper were magic as well and were in great demand by federal, state, and local police agencies throughout northern Nevada.

As for Mr. John Dellafiora, he was from a little town called Gilboa in upstate New York. He was forty-six years old, not carrying any drugs, not a wanted fugitive, and no one knows exactly why he decided to shoot it out. Later, investigators learned that Dellafiora normally carried weapons and despised law enforcement in general.

Caught in a bad situation and being pinned down in a patrol car can happen to any officer, and my son is no exception to that rule. Tragic things can happen, and situations can turn bad so fast that quite often luck is all an officer has in their corner. Thankfully, Tim had an overabundance of it on that day.

Each year on May 15th, the James D. Hoff Nevada Peace Officers Memorial in Reno holds a service where fallen Nevada Peace Officers recently killed in the line of duty are added to the memorial wall. They also recognize officers who survived dangerous situations. One day, Tim called and told me he was going to receive the James D. Hoff Memorial Survivors Award, adding, "Dad, all I did was run and scream."

I laughed and said, "That may be true, but no one runs and screams better than my son!"

On May 15th, our family, including Tim's wife Kim and his three daughters, Bailey, Ryleigh, and Kalli, witnessed Tim and Gripper receive their award. It was a very proud day for me, as Tim is one of the finest state troopers I have ever seen.

Yes, the job of a rural Nevada State trooper is as lonely as the Maytag repair man and much more dangerous, but on this day there were plenty of officers to get the job done, and no one but the instigator was killed.

License Plates, What's the Purpose?

Every workday, all day long, state troopers observe just about every little detail they can. Of particular interest are vehicles, occupants, traffic, the continual search for speeders and violators of traffic laws, DUIs, and, unfortunately, every darn license plate that goes by. I say unfortunately because after being retired for over twenty years, I still look at every darn license plate that goes by.

In 1901, New York was the first state in America to require that newfangled automobiles have an identifier. These "plates" were handcrafted by each individual owner out of metal or leather, bearing the owner's first and last initials until too many people with the same initials became confusing. Two years later, Massachusetts was the first state to issue blue and white license plates that simply said, "Mass. Automobile Identifier."

Initially, many new drivers were quite pleased with the advent of state-issued license plates, hoping that the numerous, hard-to-follow, local regulations that favored horses and wagons would be replaced by consistent state laws and uniform standards for vehicles.

Since their inception, a license plate, along with the corresponding registration certificate, identifies the vehicle it is attached to, its owner and other pertinent vehicle information. Since 1967, if that same vehicle has been reported stolen or involved in a crime or is known to be occupied by a fugitive or by the perpetrator(s) of any felony crime anywhere in America, it is entered into the National Crime

Information Center (NCIC) computer by the police agency involved. All this information is available to a law enforcement officer in a matter of seconds.

A license plate is no good to law enforcement if the plate is not visible or clearly legible. For that reason, plates are required by law to be securely attached to the vehicle, kept clean and free from foreign materials, and clearly legible. Nevada, like most states, requires license plates to be treated with a reflective material making it readable in the dark no less than 110 feet away when viewed by a vehicle equipped with normal headlights. Plastic covers that obstruct or darken the view of a license plate in any way are illegal in Nevada.

One day, I warned a woman to remove the dark plastic cover from her license plate, and she stated, "They can't be illegal because you can buy them anywhere!"

To which I replied, "Ma'am, you can buy dope anywhere, but that doesn't make it legal."

About now, you are thinking to yourself, who the heck knows these obscure license plate laws and who would care? Well, your average deputy and city officer aren't that interested, and most would not care. However, your average state trooper who has had weeks of traffic, registration, and driver's license laws beaten into them during a six-month academy do know and do care.

Initially invented for identification purposes and to keep vehicles safe from theft, it didn't take long for politicians to realize that licensing vehicles was an enormous source of revenue, thereby relegating law enforcement purposes to the backseat. Costs associated with registering vehicles vary by state, but can include sales tax, personal property tax, privilege tax, license plate fees, title transfer fees, lien recording fees, documentation fees, emission fees, electric vehicle fees, and finally, the fees involved in ordering your own personalized vanity license plate.

Yes, for a fee, you can put whatever name or word you choose on your license plate if it isn't deemed in poor taste by your state department of motor vehicles. Not only can you personalize your word or words, but they will put the witty slogan you invented on one of a multitude of different-colored, specially-designed, can't-tell-one-state-from-another license plates.

My home state of Nevada has invented dozens of these specialized plates, commemorating everything and everyone that could possibly bring in another dollar. We have special plates for full-time firemen, part-time firemen, and if they could make an extra buck, they would have them for people who wish they were firemen. There are special plates for Boy Scouts, Girl Scouts, Eagle Scouts, but not for Cub and Brownie Scouts only because they are not old enough to drive. Don't forget the special plates for street rods, classic rods, hot rods, vintage rods, antique cars, military cars, and before long, stolen cars, recalled cars, and slow-moving cars in the fast lane. Followed by active military, retired veterans, Purple Heart recipients, National Guard, Civil Air Patrol, Masons, and before long, Las Vegas mafia hitmen, garbage men, and ex-7-Eleven employees. Sadly, the list goes on.

Vanity plates with witty words are fun and not the problem. What is absurd are the dozens and dozens of specialized plates from Nevada and every other state in the union. As a young state trooper, I could look briefly at any license plate on any car and in half a second know which of the fifty states it hailed from. Now it takes much more than a glance.

We are now moving into the digital license plate era, which has been approved in several states. The digital screen, attached to the rear of your car, will show your license plate number, display messages like weather conditions, Amber Alerts, road warnings, and may even pay toll road fees. Your electronic license plate will always know the location of your car and your children as they cruise about town. The downside to digital plates is that they are expensive to buy and require a yearly maintenance fee. Rest assured that your DMV will find new ways to make money from them.

Hours from Death

L as Vegas, Nevada is by far the largest city in the Silver State. Unlike any other city in the world, it is an entertainment, gambling, and tourist mecca that draws over 40 million visitors each year. Naturally, when anyone hears that one is from Nevada, people immediately think of hot and dry Las Vegas which lies in the northern portion of the Mojave Desert. Most of the rest of Nevada lies within a very different desert that is nothing at all like Las Vegas.

North America has four major deserts. Three are hot deserts, and one is cold. Of these, the Mojave Desert at 22,000 square miles is the smallest and the hottest. It includes Death Valley and lies almost entirely within the southeastern portion of California, with small portions extending north and east into Arizona, Utah, and southern Nevada surrounding Las Vegas.

South of the Mojave lies the much larger Sonoran Desert. It is also a hot desert, approximately 120,000 square miles in size, and includes small portions of southeastern California and southwestern Arizona, with the largest portion in northwestern Mexico extending almost to the southern tip of the Baja Peninsula.

East of the Sonoran Desert is the Chihuahuan Desert. At 140,000 square miles, it is North America's largest hot desert. About half of the Chihuahuan Desert lies within the United States and includes southeastern Arizona, southern New Mexico, and western Texas. The other half is in north-central Mexico.

Comparable in size to the Chihuahuan Desert and north of the Mojave Desert lies the Great Basin Desert. The Great Basin Desert is a cold desert and covers three-quarters of the entire state of Nevada, western and southern Utah, the southern third of Idaho, and the southeastern corner of Oregon.

The Great Basin Desert is home to just about every Nevadan who does not live in or near Las Vegas, and it has been my home for most of my life. The Great Basin topography is called basin and range. The desert is comprised of wide, high-altitude valleys (most exceeding 3,900 feet in elevation) bordered by numerous mountain ranges, giving Nevada the distinction of being the most mountainous state in the lower 48 with over 300 individual named mountain ranges. The Great Basin Desert is massive, sparsely populated, and receives an average of six to twelve inches of precipitation per year, mostly in the form of snow. While rare, northern Nevada does occasionally receive snow during the summer months, and it is common for temperatures in the high mountains to drop to dangerously cold levels at night, especially when storms roll through.

People who perish in America's hot deserts usually die of hyperthermia (high body temperature from exposure to heat) and thirst. People who perish in the Great Basin Desert usually do so from hypothermia (low body temperature from exposure to the cold). It is in one of these cold, remote, Great Basin mountain ranges that this story begins.

On Thursday, May 11th, 2017, Lester and Kathy Porter decided to go for a hike in the desert mountains near Richmond Spring outside of the small town of Eureka, Nevada. They parked their car at the bottom of a hill and as they got out, they were passed by a Chevy Silverado pickup truck headed for the top of the hill. Lester, hiking ahead of his wife, arrived near the top first and overheard a man talking to a small child behind a large clump of brush.

The Porters couldn't see the man or the child but heard an engine idling, and then it began to rev loudly. The Porters walked into a clearing and were surprised to see the pickup truck burst out of the brush, speeding downhill in reverse. The truck bounced and ran into some large rocks where it stopped.

The Porters ran up to the truck and immediately saw fire inside the cab, but there was no one in it. Looking around and still not seeing anyone, they called out twice, asking, "Are you okay?"

A man answered as if nothing had happened, "Yes, I'm okay."

The man seemed so calm, and the situation so weird that the Porters thought it best to get out of there and go get help. As they were leaving, Mrs. Porter heard a small child start to cry and a man say, "Shhh, it's okay." Though quite concerned for the child, they continued with their plan to contact the authorities.

By the time the sheriff's deputy and fire truck reached the remote scene, the pickup truck was completely destroyed by fire, including the license plates, and the man and child were long gone.

On the day before, Wednesday, May 10th, six-year-old Jaylynn Dunden and seven-year-old Madison Dunden were picked up at their school in Boise, Idaho by their father, 29-year-old Joshua Dunden. Dunden was involved in an ongoing child custody case with the girl's mother which was scheduled to be settled in June. Both mother and father shared joint custody at the time, and third-hand information was relayed to Mrs. Dunden that the girls' father had taken them camping overnight, so no one was overly concerned.

On Friday, May 12th, when two days had gone by with no word from Joshua, Mrs. Dunden contacted the Boise Police Department. Since there was no evidence of a crime and the missing father and girls didn't rise to the level of issuing an Amber Alert, Boise police sent information out to Idaho law enforcement agencies, and the family posted missing persons information on the internet.

On Saturday, May 13th, Boise Police became more concerned upon learning of the father's use of illicit drugs and behavior issues, but still no major regional alert was initiated.

On Sunday, May 14th, one of Kathy Porter's friends who had heard of her and Lester's strange encounter with a man and a child near Richmond Spring on Thursday found a missing person bulletin on Facebook and brought it to Kathy's attention. When Kathy realized that the description of the pickup closely resembled the one they had seen on Thursday before it burned, she relayed the information to the Eureka County Sheriff's Office which started to organize searchers for the following day.

On Monday morning, May 15th, though little had been done by the local sheriff's office the previous four days to identify the burned truck or search for the man and children, the sheriff's office finally located one of several hidden serial numbers on the frame of the burnt truck. The Vehicle Identification Number (VIN) immediately identified it as belonging to Joshua Dunden. That set the wheels for the rest of the day in motion.

Boise Police issued an Amber Alert throughout the western region, identifying Joshua Dunden as possibly being armed and accompanied by both Madison and Jaylynn, who were believed to be in danger.

Footprints of a man and two small children were located from four days earlier which headed off into the mountains, indicating they were still in the area. Meanwhile, the sheriff continued preparing the search efforts. In rural Nevada, this is no small feat, and it would take precious hours for enough people to come together to make this happen. Numerous local and state officers were called to assist from throughout northern Nevada, including my oldest son, Nevada State Police Detective Tim Raabe.

Tim and his lieutenant, Jason Franklin, arrived mid-afternoon from

Winnemucca, two hundred miles away. They were met by a growing number of volunteers from state, federal, and local law enforcement agencies, along with ranchers on horseback, locals on ATVs, and some hikers.

An air and ground search finally began, but where to start? Looking for a man and two very small children in the high Nevada desert mountains with no idea where they got off to was like looking for the proverbial needle in the haystack. Sheriff's deputies, Tim, and his fellow detectives began following the footprints and recovered a backpack with ammunition, two rifles, knives, clothing, and other survival type tools, but finding the items of clothing was worrisome, as it meant that Dunden and the girls no longer had use of them.

The father and girls had been out in the elements for four days and nights trekking across the mountains. The weather over the last few days had been cold and overcast, and a summer storm was arriving within a few hours which would lower temperatures to deadly levels. Tracking anyone with a four-day head start is a time-sensitive process, and with daylight running short, it was not likely to produce results in time.

Around 5 p.m., ranchers Jim and Vera Baumann heard their dog barking, and Jim went to investigate. Jim walked around the corner and saw a man walking across his pasture toward the house. The man was wearing cutoff shorts, a lightweight hoodie, and no shoes. He was cold, tired, and in bad shape. The Baumanns had been alerted earlier about the missing man and children and immediately identified the man as Joshua Dunden. Vera went inside the house and called 911 to report the news. After observing that Dunden had no gun on him, Vera invited him onto the porch and brought him some hot coffee.

When Dunden was asked about the girls, he stated, "I knew we weren't going to make it and that I had better leave them and go for help."

In the preceding four days, Dunden and his two little girls had walked several miles around and to the opposite side of the large mountain range from where their truck had burned and their footprints began. Dunden had left the girls somewhere in the mountains that afternoon but didn't know where and estimated that he had walked over four miles to reach the ranch. At least the searchers now had an idea where to start looking. With several square miles of steep, rugged mountains to search and no more than a few hours of daylight left to do so, they sprang into action.

The group of deputies and detectives drove to the Baumann Ranch on the other side of the mountain range where Dunden was immediately taken into custody and the search could take place near where the girls were last seen. Their chance of surviving another night out in a storm with much colder temperatures were close to zero. And as if that weren't bad enough, these ranges were home to countless mountain lions.

Detective Tim Raabe, knowing that he would have to be running and moving fast, removed his bulletproof vest and stripped down to light clothes. With one bottle of water, a police radio, and a cell phone, he and his fellow Nevada state detectives left the ranch and proceeded across the desert to the base of the mountain. Each of the numerous ridgelines that ran toward the mountaintop were separated by steep canyons, so each of the four detectives picked ridgelines several hundred yards apart to climb and search.

As Tim moved fast up the mountain, he stopped regularly to scan the terrain and call out to the girls with no results. About an hour later, he had reached the top of the summit and called out again, "Girls, it's time to go home."

In a steep bowl below him, he heard a very faint voice reply, "Okay."

Tim could not see the girls, but he knew they were there and called to his closest partner, Detective John Cessford, who was searching the adjacent ridgeline. As John made his way over to help, Tim dropped into the steep bowl and found the girls hiding amidst large rocks covered with branches.

Both girls were barefoot, half-dressed in lightweight clothing, and suffering from severe hypothermia. They were so scratched up and torn, it looked like they had been in a fight with an alley cat. Six-year-old Jaylynn was unable to speak. She was semi-conscious, vomiting, and had no control over her bowels. Seven-year-old Madison was barely able to speak, shivering uncontrollably, and told Tim that her daddy told her not to speak to anyone, especially the police, or she would be shot. The weather had turned to sleet and rain mixed with 20-mph winds. The temperature had dropped to 32 degrees.

When Detective Cessford arrived to help, both he and Tim stripped off their shirts and wrapped them around the girls in a vain attempt to warm them up. Both men tried their police radios and cell phones to contact their colleagues for help, but they were unable to get through to anyone, which unfortunately is normal for rural Nevada.

Each man, stripped of upper clothing, picked up a girl and began the arduous task of hiking them out of the steep canyon back to the top of the ridge. After carrying the little girls two and a half miles, it was almost dark, and they still had no functioning radios or phones. Both Detective Raabe and Detective Cessford were suffering from mild hypothermia at this point and were far beyond exhausted. The detectives spotted some Bureau of Land Management rangers searching in an ATV about a mile below them, so Detective Cessford pulled his service weapon and fired three shots into the air which is a signal of distress. The BLM rangers responded and made their way over to the men as they continued down the mountain.

When the rangers met the men, they took the girls and drove for the ranch while both men, still with no upper clothing, continued walking the mile and a half to the Baumann Ranch. They were met by their supervisor, Lieutenant Franklin, and Detective Sergeant Brewer, who decided that it was way past time to get the two spent detectives their clothing back.

The girls were flown by air ambulance to a hospital where they spent the next four days recovering from multiple medical issues. Their pediatrician stated that had they not been found when they were neither would have survived the night.

The father, Joshua Dunden, was suffering from methamphetamine-fueled delusions when he picked up the girls and had told them that they were not safe from the government and others, especially the police. Luckily, seven-year-old Madison answered Tim when she heard him call out.

Every day, our law enforcement officers go to work hoping to make a difference, often never knowing the true results of their efforts. However, in this case, two dedicated detectives got lucky and then gave it everything they had to see that two beautiful little girls were reunited with their mother and lived to see another day.

Slowing Down or Stopping

State troopers are referred to as Super Troopers, Smokies, Bears, Smokey the Bear, Ramp Roosters, and AAA (Triple A) with a gun. The police powers associated with state police agencies differ across the nation, but it should come as no surprise that most of them are very well-trained in laws related to traffic, licensing of drivers, vehicle registration, vehicle theft, driving under the influence, investigating traffic accidents, and enforcing commercial vehicle safety.

Troopers have the authority to handle or investigate any crime within their state, but the rules differ greatly from state to state as to what types of crimes they normally handle. Unless asked to assist local officers, Nevada troopers do not respond to loud neighbors, barking dogs, bar fights, domestic disturbances, missing persons, robberies, and murders. If a fireman is unavailable, never call a trooper to get a cat out of a tree because there is only one way to remove it easily.

You may get away with passing a city policeman or deputy with an expired registration, shattered window, bald tire, or taillight out, but not your average state trooper because traffic is what we do. This expertise also helps when teaching young members of our own families how to drive.

I had the opportunity to ride with my grandson, Riley Houghton, who had recently obtained his learner's permit. Riley was at the wheel of his mom's large Suburban and was driving the family into the eastern Sierra Mountains in search of a Christmas tree. Riley had grown up in rural Nevada with lots of dirt roads and few cops. He had some driving experience, but like most young men his age, he liked to drive a little fast.

When we reached the windy, two-lane, mountain highway, Riley braked going into each corner and accelerated coming out as his two grandmothers, dad, mom, sister, and I swayed about. I was beside Riley in the front passenger seat as the entire car of backseat drivers rightfully complained. The Christmas trees were not going to run off before we got there, so Riley was directed to slow down.

As the day progressed, I was able to share with Riley my wealth of driving knowledge like the color and meaning of different road signs, the distance from a turn that signals are required, and the law prohibiting the use of the center turn lane to merge into traffic. The last lesson was the one he would never forget—the difference between stopping and slowing down.

After a couple of rolling stops, I asked Riley, "Do you truly understand the difference between coming to a complete stop versus just slowing down?"

"Yes, I think I do," he answered.

"If you pull over for a minute, I will teach you the difference."

Riley pulled over, stopped, and looked at me. I smiled at him, reached across the center console, and began gently slapping him across the face, alternating cheeks. As I continued slapping, I asked him, "Now, do you want me to stop or do you want me to slow down?"

Riley smiled at me and said, "I think I get it!"

I stopped slapping, smiled at him, and said, "Good. If you remember that lesson, you will never roll through a stop sign and accidentally pull out in front of another vehicle."

Riley's dad Tim gave a big hearty laugh and said, "That was great. I don't think Riley will ever forget that driving lesson!"

We had a nice day in the mountains cutting a Christmas tree, and Riley, a young man I greatly admire, drove us all home safely.

All Good Things Come to an End

Two books filled with stories from my career have come to an end, and it has been fun sharing them with you. My intentions were to write interesting true stories that would give all of you a much better understanding of the duties, experiences, humor, sadness, and dangers of being a rural state trooper in the western United States. Since my first book, *Patrolling the Heart of the West*, was released over five years ago, I have received countless positive comments from readers who claim to have a much better understanding of the different duties and calls for service state troopers perform, so it appears that my goals have been met.

Looking back on my life, I realize that there were an unlimited number of occupations I could have chosen, many of which paid a lot more, but I absolutely loved my job. Putting my uniform on every day and patrolling the highways of my home state as a trooper and as a traffic sergeant rarely seemed like work. The work portion of my career began when I accepted the position of personnel sergeant and transferred into headquarters, followed by six years as an operational lieutenant. Both of those positions were interesting and satisfying, but they were a lot more work than fun.

Prior to accepting the personnel sergeant position, I was a swing-shift sergeant in the city of Reno. While it was great fun and exciting running around and supervising state troopers in a busy city, I rarely saw my wife and children. I left for work in the early afternoon before any of them got home from their busy days and I returned home after they were already in bed. With Fridays and Saturdays off, the only time I had to spend with my family each week was from Friday night until midday Sunday, so accepting the personnel sergeant position at NHP Headquarters in Carson City was an easy decision.

I worked as a personnel sergeant for two years, and it was a very busy, hectic, never-catch-up, learning experience. I was responsible for monitoring and overseeing the hiring and firing of all highway patrol employees statewide, but my main job was filling two academies per year with quality applicants, which was an unbelievable amount of work. Thankfully, I had access to a hard-working highway patrol administrative assistant by the name of Patty Davis. Our days were filled with planning, scheduling, and performing all aspects associated with hiring new troopers, including recruiting, qualifying applications, physical agility testing, cognitive testing, overseeing extensive background investigations of each applicant, oral interviews, polygraph examinations, psychological written exams, in-person psychological interviews, and final selection.

Two years later, I was promoted to lieutenant. As you learned in an earlier story, the captain I was assigned to work for wanted his buddy as lieutenant instead of me, so I was relegated as the lieutenant in charge of no one and became the best darn paper clip counter in the history of the highway patrol. Lucky for me, the colonel remedied the situation, so I was able to do my job unhindered.

Lieutenant was a good job in many ways, but most of the time was spent on administrative duties with very little time on the highway. Days were filled with special assignments, operational plans for upcoming events, handling internal and external complaints, personnel problems, scheduling training, acting as liaison to local fire departments, governments, police agencies, hospitals, courts, and dealing with everything else that comes along with supervising six sergeants and sixty troopers in a large city.

So how did it all end? As you recall, after my first stint as Reno Urban Commander I was assigned as an assistant to the Director of the Department of Public Safety, Mr. James Weller, for a period of one year. Mr. Weller had been both an officer in the United States Marine Corps and an FBI agent who'd finished his long career as the Special Agent in Charge of the Las Vegas Office. James Weller was an excellent leader. After I finished my year in the director's office, I was reassigned to my previous position as the Reno/North Lake Tahoe district commander. Sadly for my entire department, Mr. Weller retired.

Unfortunately, in a matter of weeks my department changed. Fear and intimidation became the new motivational methods, and meetings went from how we were going to improve to who was going to be disciplined for daring to speak out against the new regime, especially our union representatives. There are good leaders in this world, but sadly there are others who couldn't lead a trail of ants to a picnic. Unfortunately for me, Captain Paper Clip fit in perfectly with the new regime and was promoted to Major Paper Clip.

I had several issues with the new command over the next year. One had to do with an upper-level commander, who had no experience as a highway patrol trooper, calling me an idiot in the middle of a meeting over the application of a DUI law that I knew very well and he didn't know at all. The biggest disappointment was that the other commanders in attendance knew I was right, but like scared sheep they never said a word. When I met with our local deputy district attorney to get his opinion on the matter, his exact words to me were, "Lieutenant Raabe, you are right. But if you value your job, don't ever tell the people who now run your department that they are wrong!"

Each week seemed to become a repeat of the 'You're lying to the public' motorcycle incident, and it was clear that my days were numbered.

My wife's business was booming, so I decided to retire from a career that I absolutely loved. I drove to Carson City and advised our colonel (the chief), an outstanding man who I greatly admired, of my decision. My colonel said, "I understand, Lieutenant Raabe. I can't protect any of my commanders from these people."

After the meeting with the colonel, I appeared in Carson City Justice Court on a case against a woman I had arrested for DUI the preceding year. After that, I cleaned out my patrol car and parked it for the last time in front of my office. My bride picked me up at my office and drove me home, which was a good thing because it was difficult to see through the tears in my eyes. I certainly wish my career would have ended better, however, there are no sour grapes. Except for the last year, it was a wonderful career, and I would recommend it to anyone interested.

Eventually, the regime was removed from power, but during their three-year reign the *Northern Nevada Business Weekly* newspaper reported that 100 out of 424 sworn officers and 90% of the command staff left the highway patrol. My colonel lasted a month longer than I did before retiring, stating to the *Business Weekly* afterward, "I wasn't about to sell my soul just to keep that job." By the time my son Tim followed in my footsteps three years later, the highway patrol had new leadership and was sailing along smoothly again.

For those of you who are currently managing employees or who plan to do so in the future, remember that they are your greatest asset. If you care for them, treat them with respect, encourage and assist them to do their best, and protect them from human vultures, in most instances they will take care of you and make you look better in the eyes of your bosses than you probably are.

Afterword

After retiring from the Nevada Highway Patrol, Janelle and I worked at our pond business for two years until our twenty-year-old daughter, Corrie Jo, was struck down by a very serious neurological disorder resulting from a mosquito bite (very possibly my next book). Corrie came down with West Nile Virus, which turned into a disease called Acute Disseminated Encephalomyelitis. After spending three weeks in a very large Phoenix hospital with three doctors (an internist, a neurologist, and an infectious disease specialist) who could not figure out what was wrong, Corrie was transferred by ambulance to a specialty hospital called the Barrow Neurological Institute. Corrie's team of doctors at Barrow were the very best. They finally figured out what was wrong with her but told us that if they saved our beautiful daughter's life, she would never be the same. Miraculously, after ten long months of decline, they did save her life, but sadly she never fully recovered and was left with permanent, life-altering deficiencies. This event really took the wind out of our sails, and it has been a lifelong struggle ever since. In 2004, we left our pond business into the hands of one of our longtime employees and moved back to Winnemucca.

In 2005 I decided to run for Humboldt County Sheriff. Years before, as a brand-new highway patrol lieutenant, I was lucky enough to attend and successfully complete Northwestern University's School of Police Staff and Command. This difficult three-month school prepares law enforcement officers in all aspects of law enforcement administration. I had the training, the experience, and the desire to be sheriff, so I gave it a try. I served the first thirteen years of my law enforcement career in Winnemucca, but I moved away for twelve years to gain the knowledge and experience needed to become the sheriff. Ultimately, my absence proved to be too long, and I lost the election by a total of sixty-nine votes.

Janelle and I are whitewater rafters, and since losing the sheriff's race, we have rafted almost every major river in the western United States, many of them multiple times. Had I won the election, I would not have eight trips driving a raft down the mighty Colorado River through the Grand Canyon. Each trip being a three-week, 280-mile-long adventure through one of the most fascinating places on earth.

Janelle and I have been married for thirty-six years. We live in Sparks, Nevada during the summer and Yuma, Arizona during the winter where we own two Papa Murphy's pizza stores. We stay quite busy working a little, traveling a lot, and playing as much as we can. We have a wonderful life and enjoy our time together.

Our oldest son, Tim, is currently a Nevada State Police sergeant stationed in Winnemucca. He and his wife, Kim, gave us three granddaughters—Bailey, Ryleigh, and Kalli—and as of now, one great-granddaughter, Avery. Our middle son, Mike, is a retired Air Force fighter pilot and now flies for Delta Airlines. He and his wife, Mandy, provided us with two grandsons, Spencer and Carson (the wild driver from my last book) and two granddaughters, Katie and Megan. Our daughter, Corrie, gave birth to a son, Tyler, and a daughter, Carley, but was unable to raise either of them. Tyler is being raised by his father, Doug, and our granddaughter, Carley, was adopted at birth by my first cousin, Jennifer, and her husband, Tim. Jennifer and Tim are our new kids, and their older son, Riley, is our grandson as well. So, we have four kids and their spouses, ten grandchildren, one great-grandchild, and all are wonderful. Like my mom, Charlotte, used to say, "Every old crow thinks her children are the blackest!"

I want to thank my editor, Jon Gosch, for his support, expertise, guidance, and patience; Latah Books of Spokane, Washington for publishing my work; retired Nevada State trooper, Cobb County police officer, and good friend, Mike Sigman, for writing and contributing the story, "A Horrible End to a Wonderful Career"; my wife Janelle for her love and encouragement; and to each one of you for showing the interest and taking the time to read my books. It has been an enjoyable and rewarding experience to write and share these true stories with all of you!

Sincerely,

Steven E. Raabe
Nevada Highway Patrol ID #3067 (Retired)
Email: snowraabe@gmail.com

www.ingramcontent.com/pod-product-compliance
Lightning Source LLC
Chambersburg PA
CBHW021618120626
46545CB00001B/287